MILITARY MODELLING GUIDE TO SOLO WARGAMING

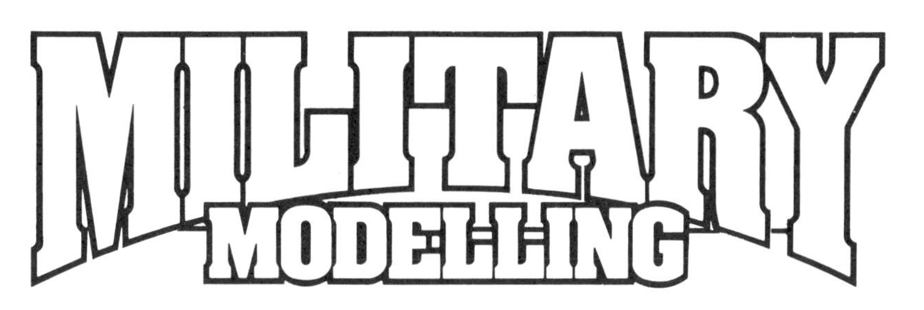

GUIDE TO SOLO WARGAMING

STUART ASQUITH

ARGUS BOOKS

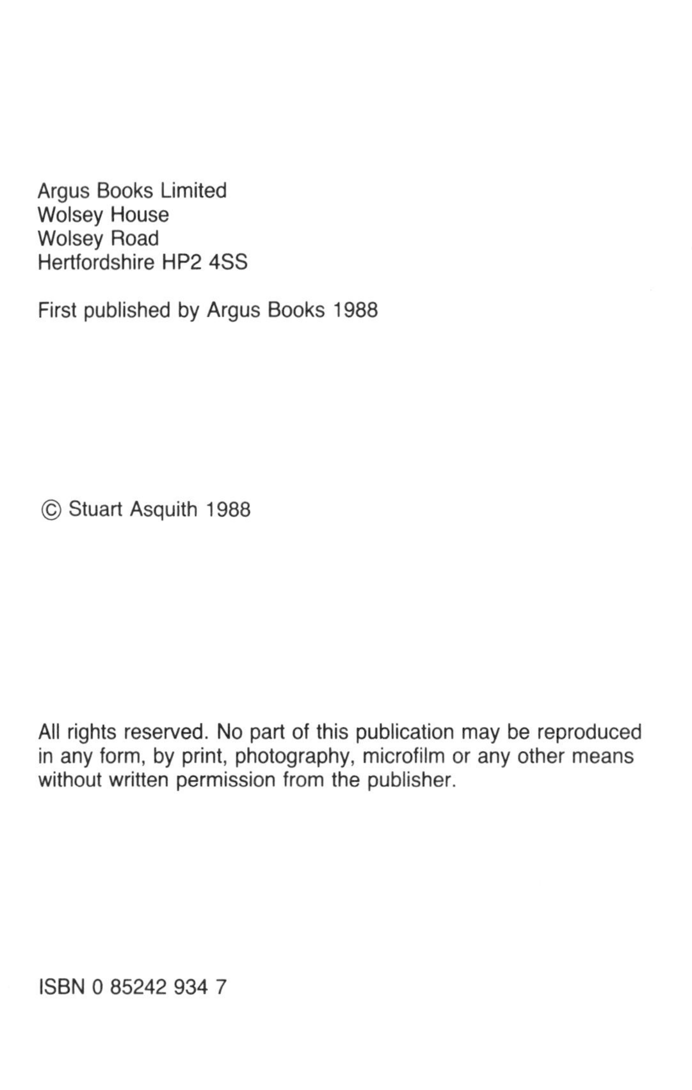

Argus Books Limited
Wolsey House
Wolsey Road
Hertfordshire HP2 4SS

First published by Argus Books 1988

ISBN 0 85242 934 7

Photosetting by Alan Sutton Publishing Ltd, Gloucester
Printed and bound by LR Printing Services Ltd.
Manor Royal, Crawley, West Sussex, RH10 2QN, England.

CONTENTS

On the cover: Mid 18th century 30mm soldiers advance to do battle (from the author's collection).

ACKNOWLEDGEMENTS

The author would like to thank the many people who have helped in the production of this book.

Particular thanks are due to Rab MacWilliam and Folly Marland of Argus Books, and to Ken Jones, the Editor of *Military Modelling* magazine for all their help and encouragement.

Also, to my good friend Charles S. Grant, not only for his continued support, but for his more than generous permission to quote from one of his own books, and to John Bennett, founder of The Solo Wargamers Association.

Finally, my sincere thanks to Beryl and Linda, who between them managed the minor miracle of converting my scribble into pages of neatly typed manuscript.

1 THE REASONS FOR PLAYING SOLO WARGAMES

Wargaming as a hobby or pastime continues to grow in popularity. While perhaps not enjoying a repetition of the heady expansion which took place in the 1970s, wargaming still attracts an increasing number of adherents. This is particularly the case over the last decade, when fantasy wargaming has been responsible for bringing many newcomers into the hobby.

It is difficult to offer a precise figure when attempting to quantify the size of the hobby today, but reasonable estimates would seem to indicate that wargamers must number in thousands throughout the United Kingdom and ten times this figure worldwide.

As wargaming attracts more people, the number of wargame clubs and societies has also increased. There are few towns in the UK that do not have a club in one form or another, with a membership of anything from a dozen to a hundred people. Such groups are the building blocks of the hobby and have contributed a great deal to its continuance. Many of the larger and more enterprising clubs run their own wargame conventions which are always popular and well supported. Indeed, by far the greater number of such events are now run by clubs – and very well too, generally speaking.

As the hobby increases, so too does the number of related commercial and amateur enterprises. The companies which produce wargames figures continually increase their ranges and nowadays there are very few periods of history for which the wargamer cannot buy figures. Perhaps the biggest increase is in the number of companies prepared either to paint the customer's chosen figures or to provide ready-painted wargamer armies. Charging fairly high prices – inevitable when one considers the labour-intensive nature of the work involved – such companies offer figures ready for instant use on the wargames table. The proliferation of these painting services underlines the demand that must exist for them throughout the hobby.

The rule writers, too, have been busy. Popular published sets of rules are, apparently, constantly in need of what is euphemistically referred to as 'revision' by their writers and are re-issued at intervals as the 'new and fully revised edition'. Rather than being an actual revision of the original, such sets are in fact usually completely new. Other sets of rules are rather more carefully thought out, however, and seldom receive such cavalier attention from their authors. Properly produced and reliable, such rules are deservedly popular with the more discerning type of wargamer who is unmoved by the razzmatazz which invariably accompanies the publication of the latest edition of a commercial set of rules.

No one existing set of wargame rules enjoys universal acclaim throughout the hobby, despite the many claims to the contrary by their various authors. For obvious financial reasons, it would be good news indeed for one set of rules to be named as the definitive publication. Fortunately, it is extremely unlikely that this will ever happen, for there are more than enough free-thinking wargamers to counter the sheep-like mentalities who would permit such an event to occur. It is without doubt that such a move would sound the death knell of the hobby by both stultifying its progress and preventing its expansion. Some wargame clubs tend to impose a particular set of rules, be they commercial or home produced, as standard within the club. This can produce the same effect on a smaller scale and such clubs are fortunate indeed to retain their members.

There have been many attempts to 'organise' the hobby, all so far without success – fortunately so, in my view. The numerous, often conflicting but seldom thought-out proposals usually involve the vague formation of national or regional bodies to 'guide and regulate' the hobby. Once again, as long as there are free-thinking wargamers in the hobby, such attempts at regimentation will always be resisted.

From a certain, admittedly cynical, viewpoint then, today's wargaming can be identified as a somewhat breathless and increasingly commercialised hobby, with minority attempts at its 'organisation' hovering ineffectually on the fringe.

So, what can be done – is today's hobby beyond redemption? The answer clearly is no, it is not. Many wargamers are more than happy with the hobby and derive much enjoyment from it. The purpose of this book, however, is to offer a viable alternative should any of the foregoing ring true with the reader.

While there are many wargamers who belong to clubs, there is at least an equal number who either prefer not to join a club or do not have access to one. For both these types of player it is modestly suggested that solo wargaming will succeed in filling a gap in the hobby for them. There are many advantages to being a solo wargamer and I hope that this book will cover most of them.

A wargamer does not necessarily have to be domiciled either in the remote north of Scotland or the furthest tip of England to be isolated in the hobby. Lacking transport, perhaps the nearest club remains inaccessible, or even if this were not the case, the prevalent attitude which exists there may not be to the wargamer's own taste. Then, too, there are those who find any commercialism in the hobby a deterrent, which is avoided if the wargamer plays solo games.

Solo wargaming can offer a viable alternative to playing a 'live' opponent and in some cases can prove to be a positive bonus. The wargamer who solos from choice enjoys perhaps the very best of the hobby, since the involvement is total. While clubs and conventions can be visited if and when required, any activity in the hobby always remains at a very personal level.

This personal aspect of the hobby cannot be overstated. A wargamer's armies are purchased with his own money and painted in his own time to his own ability, taste and research. Now, one of the unfortunate and seemingly unavoidable by-products of a wargames convention can be the opinionated ridicule which is both freely and frequently given out by a minority of self-styled, self-appointed 'experts'. While helpful comment can undoubtedly be of value, 'expert' advice of this nature most certainly is not. All wargamers put a part of themselves into their armies and they can become very personal possessions. Thus, an army kept out of the public gaze can have its organisation amended according to the wargamer's ideas and continuing research, without any disparaging remarks or external and unwanted influences. This last is an important point. How many wargamers have raised armies in a given period, not simply because they personally wish to, but due to the fact that their club wargames that period? All too often the projects and periods that the wargamer actually wishes to follow up are pushed aside.

This is not the case for the solo wargamer, however, for he is in total control of the periods covered by his armies. The soloist can afford to become fully absorbed in a particular army or theatre of war, researching it and wargaming it to the full.

Above all, perhaps, the solo wargamer has the full advantage of time – time to consider all the aspects of a particular campaign, time to plan and re-think wargame rule mechanisms and time to mull over a particular situation as it arises. There is no problem with wargame opponents having the 'eleven o'clock twitch' as reserves are recklessly committed and charges declared with one eye on the clock, as work and the real world looms on the morrow.

Further, the 'regular' wargamer cannot always conjure up an opponent at short notice, so spontaneous games are sometimes difficult to arrange. The solo player on the other hand can put on a game at any time – impromptu battles, say, on a Sunday morning or late at night present no problems.

Clearly, however, no matter how keen the potential soloist may be, ideas for games and game mechanisms are needed before solo battles or campaigns can be conducted. This book sets out to provide just that sort of information, either by creating new systems or adapting existing ones. While some of the suggestions set out in the following pages may be familiar to some readers, many of them are new and are offered as a basis for adaptation, alteration and extension as required by the solo player.

2 SOLO WARGAMING SYSTEMS

Irrespective of the period in which the soloist intends to wargame, or the manner in which the games are to be conducted, various solo mechanisms and techniques will be needed.

Either prior to any action taking place or during the game itself – at whatever level it is pitched – devices are required in order that the solo player can introduce a random element into the unfolding situation. The following ideas are offered for consideration by the reader to accept, modify or reject as is seen fit. They can be used either in isolation or in conjunction with one another to insert whatever degree of disruption is required.

Chance Cards

It is a well-established dictum that war should be regared as an art rather than as a science. To reflect this, on the tabletop the solo player has a number of options open to him and one of these is the use of chance cards.

In its simplest form, the chance card is a means of interjecting a degree of uncertainty into the control of a game, leaving the wargamer to react as required. The variations on the contents of chance cards are practically without limit, for they can be made to affect people, places, supplies, battle conditions, weather, organisation or any manner of things. Further, they can be based on personal or impersonal, strategical or tactical aspects.

Chance cards can reflect both serious military alternatives or problems as well as situations which are set in a somewhat lighter vein. Further, they may be employed singly or in multiples and introduced either every game move or at whatever interval is deemed to suit the particular situation.

It is as well to now offer some suggestions as to the possible content of typical chance cards before discussing their implications and effect on a wargame.

For example, let us imagine a chance card which bears the

legend 'Mistress of the General Officer Commanding discovered in the arms of the Senior Cavalry Commander'. Here is an opportunity for the wargamer to pursue various trains of thought. Does the General demand satisfaction and challenge the Cavalry Commander to a duel – if so, does he win or lose? Perhaps the General will have a fit of anger and have the Cavalry Officer summarily shot out of hand, or perhaps dismiss him from his important post in the army, sending him back to headquarters in disgrace.

What effect does all this have on the cavalry and as a direct result the entire army? Is the Senior Cavalry Commander's deputy a capable officer or a bit of a duffer? Can he handle the responsibility suddenly thrust on him? What effect will all this have on the cavalry? Are the rank and file bothered about the dealings of the 'top brass' or will they simply do their duty whoever's hand is at the helm?

Thus, it can be seen that the 'knock-on' effect of one simple sentence on a chance card can be considerable. It all really depends on the imagination, ingenuity and requirements of the solo wargamer.

While the following sample chance cards are listed under separate headings, the implications and results from many of them can influence several different aspects either simultaneously or progressively.

1. MOVEMENT

A. STRATEGICAL

1. Light infantry cavalry screen, operating in front of the army, lose contact with their main force.
2. The artillery train takes the wrong route and becomes lost. One division of the army is delayed and falls behind.

B. TACTICAL

1. Supporting artillery becomes bogged down and cannot advance.
2. Courier taking orders from Commanding Officer is killed.
3. Enemy slip undetected past sentry posts.

2. SUPPLY

A. STRATEGICAL

1. Artillery supply column ambushed by irregulars and halted.
2. Food supplies found to be contaminated, rendering them unusable.

B. TACTICAL

1. Wrong calibre ammunition supplied to some batteries of field guns.
2. Infantry in the IV division have only one round left each.

3. PERSONALITIES

A. STRATEGICAL

1. The King, plagued by gout, irrationally orders the dispersion of his armies.
2. One of the countries allied to your own joins the enemy.

B. TACTICAL

1. Your chief infantry and artillery commanders are not on speaking terms and refuse to co-operate with one another.
2. Due to language problems, your division of auxiliary infantry misunderstand their orders and fall back.

4. GENERAL

A. STRATEGICAL

1. Cavalry reserve is badly positioned and cannot deploy to support the army.
2. The weather breaks overnight and heavy rain reduces the few roads that do exist to mud-baths.

B. TACTICAL

1. Cavalry reserve is badly positioned and cannot deploy to support the army.
2. Light cavalry screen fails to identify enemy units and their strength as a result is miscalculated.
3. Continuous rain dampens your men's muskets/ bowstrings rendering them useless.

If the above suggestions are judged perhaps to reflect problems set largely in the Horse and Musket period, i.e. 1600–1852, then they require only minor changes to make them suitable for any period.

Ammunition, for example, can be assumed to refer to anything from javelins to fragmentation grenades, and cannon balls to surface – to – surface missiles. Cavalry can in turn be seen as actual horsemen or as armoured vehicles, while the infantry can be Roman, Medieval, Renaissance or Modern.

The whole purpose is to offer the wargamer problems to solve – the period in which they are set is of a secondary nature.

The negative nature of the statements can equally readily become positive to give the wargamer's forces – or those of the enemy – some good news for a change.

How about your supporting cavalry finding a good road, merely speeding up their approach, or capturing some enemy artillery ammunition, e.g. fused shells for the howitzers or stones for your ballistae, enabling your forces to increase their rate of fire? After all, not all news is bad news, even on the battlefield! Here again is another variable for the wargamer to explore – how many negative/positive chance cards to have available, and in what ratio.

When the cards are drawn and acted upon depends on the player and his needs for the current campaign. To draw one card at the start of every game move could be to take the idea a shade too far perhaps, unless a fair number of the cards are blank, thus posing no problems. Again the ratio of blanks to actual will need to be decided upon and can of course be varied to suit the needs of a particular set-up.

Alternatively, all the chance cards could have problems on them, but the player only draws one, say, every fourth move. It can often happen that the situation caused by the drawing of one card is still being resolved by the soloist when the time/move arrives to draw another. Problems on problems could result.

The cards themselves are simple enough to make. The wargamer can use playing cards and place suitably-sized sticky labels (the peel-off variety one can buy at any stationer's) on their surface. On this label can be written – or typed, if you know someone with this ability – the required message.

Alternatively, players can easily make their own chance cards using pieces of cardboard cut to suitable dimensions, say 4in. × 3in. (100mm × 75mm). Again the required message is written straight on to the surface of the card or via a label.

Dicing

Another method of interjecting uncertainty into a solo wargame is the use of dice when deciding the outcome of a situation. Let us assume for the purposes of illustration that your cavalry, scouting ahead of the main army, have reported sighting a considerable-sized body of enemy troops. Now, it matters little whether you are a Roman commander and your auxiliary cavalry have sighted Ancient Britons, or an American cavalry troop commander whose Crow scouts have detected a war party of Cheyenne warriors, the problems resulting from the sighting need to be resolved. When using dice as a means to resolve such a situation, all the possible resultant permutations need to be assessed and the likelihood of each occurring established. This will then form the basis of a 'results chart' from which a decision can be made. For example, if the possibility of the Roman commander taking an aggressive stance against the approaching hordes is deemed to be very likely, then there should be a high chance of this happening. This can be reflected by using, say, two ordinary six-sided dice and stipulating that a score of six or more results in the Romans hastily adopting battle positions.

Alternatively, if the Roman officer is likely to decide that discretion is the better part of valour and withdraw his men in some haste, the spread of dice results should make it difficult for the Romans – or U.S. cavalry – to stand. To continue the example of using two ordinary dice, then a score of four or less would be required for the regulars to stay and make a fight of it – any other score and they high-tail it into the sunset.

Many factors will influence the final outcome and any or all of them need to be considered by the solo player. The relevant factors can be viewed under set headings – Morale, Terrain, Situation etc. – plus any other points thought to be worthy of inclusion prior to arriving at a decision.

The following ideas are offered as examples of the type of input the soloist can use. Morale – are the troops regular, auxiliary or mercenary, veterans or recruits, are they well fed or on half rations, are they confident or apprehensive? Further – is the immediate terrain suitable for making a stand or taking the offensive or would a position further back (or to the left/right/etc.) be more suitable?

Finally an assessment of the overall situation – do they want to fight, how will it suit the campaign, is it better in the wider context to cut and run no matter how ignoble or irksome it may appear in the short term?

Clearly the permutations are endless and need to be assessed to suit the immediate needs of the situation. Once the 'fors' and 'againsts' have been considered, it is a fairly simple matter to reflect them proportionally with a dice score, along the lines of the two examples quoted above. Needless to say, the dice do not always oblige and an action may have to be fought, even on the most unfavourable terms to one or the other combatant, perhaps even to both.

Once the principle of dice-controlled probability is appreciated, the concept can readily be adapted to virtually any wargame situation, large or small.

Further, only regular six-sided dice have been considered here, though as the reader is doubtless aware there are literally dozens of different types of dice available. Each offers a varying range of numbers and results and can be utilised by the player as required.

Indeed, different types of dice can be used to govern the requisite range of variables. A pair of the 20-sided percentage dice, for example, will produce a range of numbers 00 to 99, while a six-sided average dice marked 2, 3, 3, 4, 4, 5 offers 4 to 10 when used with another of the same ilk.

To resolve one situation the soloist can use one type of dice, while for another a completely different type can be used. There is no rule to say that the dice used must be consistent!

Other Random Devices

While chance cards and dice readily present themselves as a means of introducing the random element, there are other methods available to the solo player. Random devices are many and varied and range from the simplistic toss of a coin to the complex random number generator. Much depends on what the soloist wants to achieve in the game as to what method and hence what degree of complication is employed. There is a great deal of merit in assessing a situation, noting possible outcomes/variables on slips of paper and drawing one from the proverbial hat.

Other members of the family can be used. Once the wargamer has listed the possible outcomes/variables of a situation, say from one to ten, another member of the household can be asked to call out a number in that range and there is the outcome decided for you.

Tables of printed random numbers can be purchased, with a pin or the tip of a pencil being used to select any one on a sheet. Care should be taken here to ensure that the range of the result options falls within that of the random numbers. The toy 'spinner' – an eight or ten or twelve edged circular piece of card pierced by a cocktail stick – can also be used, as can numbered chits or cards in a bag or box.

Doubtless other methods of obtaining random results for whatever purpose will present themselves to the solo player.

Random Terrain Methods

Generally speaking, the terrain over which a solo battle is fought will usually be dictated by a map – real or fictional (more of which later) – if one is in use. If, however, terrain is required for a 'one-off' battle then once again a degree of random selection can be used.

Two methods will be looked at here but many more will occur to the player.

Firstly, the required number of terrain items – hills, villages, trees etc.– can either be assembled or diced for. Much will depend on the overall setting of the wargame – it is of little use for example in assembling over a dozen scenic items if the battle is set in a desert context. The player can either collect up, say, a dozen items and dice to see how many are actually used, either by a set score on two ordinary dice or assuming that each item requires a dice score of 5 or 6 before it can be utilised. Alternatively, the dice themselves can decide how many pieces of scenery are selected. The score on two ordinary or perhaps average dice can be taken as the number of terrain items that can be used. This can, of course, be tailored to fit within certain required limits. Secondly, the placing of the selected items can be diced for. Either mentally or on a piece of paper the playing area can be divided up into a convenient number of squares – 12 or 6 for ordinary dice usage, 10 or 5 for average dice, 10 for a percentage dice and so on. Each piece of terrain then has an appropriate dice thrown for it and is placed in the square relative to the dice score. Fig. 1 will help to clarify this.

The same system can equally apply to other items of terrain, such as hills, farms etc., but roads and rivers need special attention if they are to follow realistic, not to say continuous, courses. Here the dice outcomes will have to be 'fudged' or 'adjusted' where necessary, for credibility.

Troop Dispositions

Much the same type of technique can be utilised for the deployment of troops once the terrain has been laid out.

Figure 1

Let us assume that there are six items of terrain to be located:

A. Copse B. House C. Length of walling

D. Rocks E. Lichen F. Ruins

Two ordinary dice are thrown for the siting of each piece and the sample scores are as follows:

Copse 2 House 3 Walling 3

Rocks 9 Lichen 7 Ruins 8

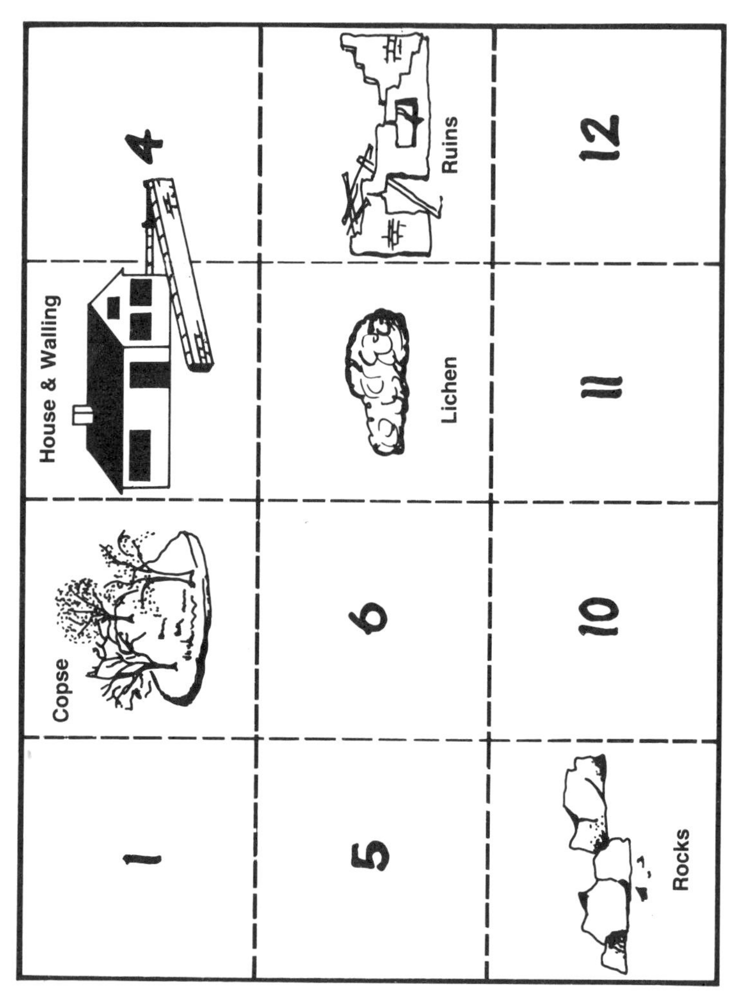

Thus the playing area would look like the diagram below. Hardly a balanced terrain and probably not one a General would have chosen to fight over. Thus the Soloist has problems straight away as the game unfolds.

Figure 2

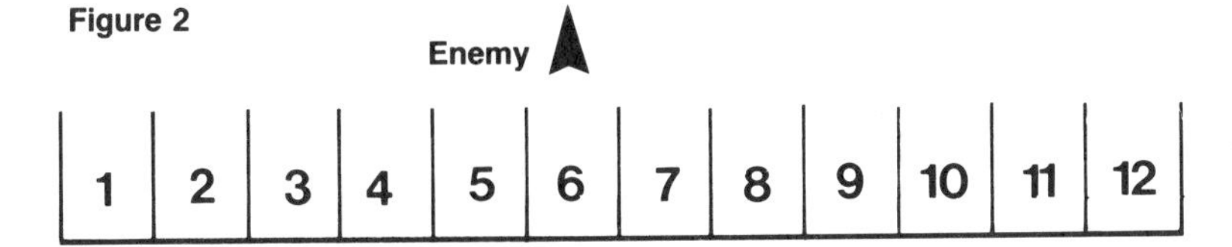

'Home' edge of table

The units can be identified and one or two dice as appropriate thrown for them to govern their placement on the table top. In this instance, however, only one edge of the table is subdivided into suitable intervals. Fig. 2 will underline one suggested version of this method.

Now to take the example a stage further, let us assume we are setting up a Horse and Musket game of the Napoleonic period.

Your force is as follows: six regiments of line infantry, one of light infantry, one of light cavalry, three of heavy cavalry and two field guns.

Two ordinary dice are thrown for each unit and we will assume for the purposes of the exercise that the following scenes resulted:

1st LINE INFANTRY REGT.	7	1st LIGHT INFANTRY REGT.	5
2nd " " "	3	1st LIGHT CAVALRY "	5
3rd " " "	2	1st HEAVY CAVALRY "	4
4th " " "	8	2nd HEAVY CAVALRY "	11
5th " " "	4	3rd HEAVY CAVALRY "	6
6th " " "	4	1st FIELD GUN	3
		2nd FIELD GUN	12

Thus the deployment of the troops would appear as in Fig. 3.

Again, hardly an ideal deployment. The soloist has to decide whether to attack (or defend as appropriate) in this formation or attempt at least a partial re-shuffle of his forces in the face of the enemy and prior to any action. Problems!

Figure 3

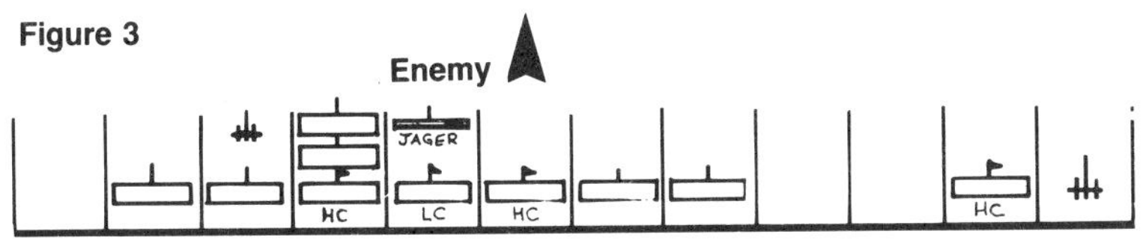

Own base line

Naturally, the same method can be inflicted on the 'enemy' leaving 'them' with much the same problem, unless the dice are co-operative and they rarely are, in my experience.

A second method is to write the names and/or types of unit on a piece of card or paper. Then add a number – the same, or perhaps twice as many, or whatever – of blank pieces. Shuffle or mix them all up and lay them out – face down of course, so that any writing is hidden – in a typical deployment suitable for both terrain and the particular game in question.

The cards or pieces of paper are then turned over *in situ* and the blanks removed. The remaining cards indicate where the wargame units are to be deployed, usually with numerous attendant problems again.

Another method of effecting deployment is to allow each side its full contingent of units or troops. Then, either before or after deployment, a number of units as dictated by the score on the appropriate number and/or type of dice is immediately removed and the army left to fight without them.

On similar lines, I well remember a solo scenario based on a Vietnam campaign in which an armed reconnaissance was to be carried out by American troops against a suspected Viet Cong stronghold.

A pleasant evening was spent pondering the composition of the force that was to be used and plans were carefully drawn up. At the very moment of departure, a chance card drawn from the stack dictated that three valuable members of the recce team had to be stood down to make room for a three man news-team which 'Washington' had decreed must accompany the mission. Not only were valuable troops denied to the Americans, but men had also to be detailed to look after the news-team.

Thus it doesn't necessarily have to be an entire army whose deployment can be amended by chance methods; small patrols can also be made to suffer – or even perhaps benefit – from the vagaries of the dice.

We shall now look at one final method of chance to insert a degree of unreliability into proceedings. So far, we have basically assumed that all the units are in more or less the right place at the right time. Granted, some units have been whisked off the table prior to any action, but generally speaking so far all the units gather simultaneously. What then, if some units fail to arrive at the battlefield, or turn up late or in the wrong place?

Firstly we can consider the approach march of units to the battle area. How many of these units get lost and never arrive, how many arrive late – and perhaps in the wrong place and so on?

To examine these possibilities in some sort of sequence, let us consider the non-arrival of troops. Although this is much the same as removing units from a laid-out battle, it does offer the added 'twist', if you will, in that the soloist is never totally sure as to which elements will fail to arrive.

Assume, then, that units are moving 'off-table' but towards the scene of the pending battle. Such movement would be monitored on maps and thus can be readily recorded. Dice would be thrown for every move on the map, either with a constant chance of troops becoming lost or an increasing/diminishing one as required.

Thus, perhaps, any unit throwing any 'double' on the dice, i.e. two threes or two fives or whatever, could be deemed to be 'lost' and removed from the reckoning for the battle. Failing that, perhaps a score of between two and four – assuming the use of two ordinary dice – could be used for the same end.

The simulation of lateness in arrival is relatively simple to implement. Using an appropriate dice, simply roll for which move sees the arrival of the unit in question.

Either mechanism gives a degree of uncertainty making any battle plans fluid, to say the least. By using both in conjunction with one another the solo player has a situation wherein it is uncertain when the units will arrive if indeed at all.

The third option in this sequence is the arrival of troops in the wrong place on the table top. This can be represented by the battle area being divided up in much the same manner as discussed for the setting up of terrain features, with some minor differences.

It is unlikely that troops will suddenly materialise in the middle of the battlefield, so it is really only the edges of the table that are being considered in this instance. There does seem a reasonable chance, however, that units will appear not only on the flanks of the action but also perhaps behind the enemy forces.

Now the table edge can be subdivided into sections, each with a fairly equal chance of having troops arrive in them. Fig. 4 illustrates this.

Thus any unit nearing the action having a dice score of '4' thrown for them would appear in the back right hand corner section as the approaching troops view the table.

A variant which could be used here is to make the arrival more likely at the 'home' or near baseline and less likely the further away towards the enemy one moves. The table would then be divided as in Fig. 5.

Figure 4

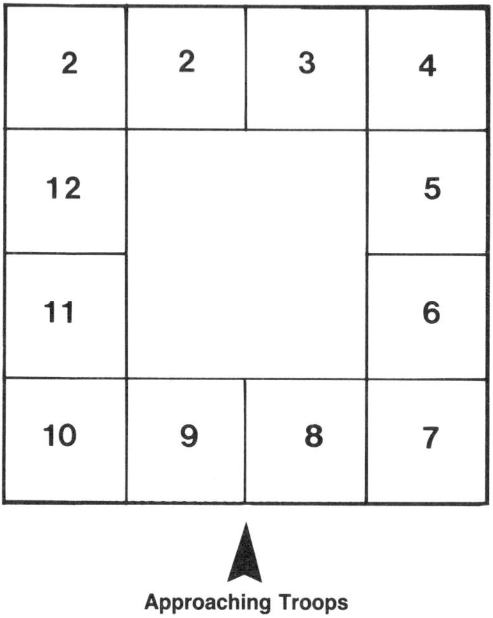

2	2	3	4
12			5
11			6
10	9	8	7

Approaching Troops

Figure 5

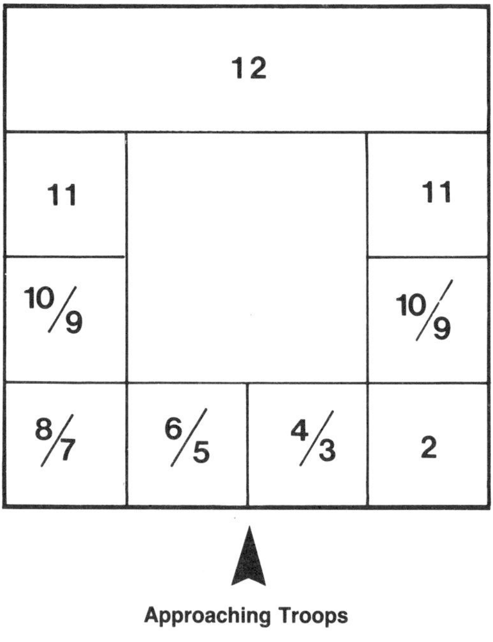

<table>
<tr><td colspan="4">12</td></tr>
<tr><td>11</td><td></td><td></td><td>11</td></tr>
<tr><td>10/9</td><td></td><td></td><td>10/9</td></tr>
<tr><td>8/7</td><td>6/5</td><td>4/3</td><td>2</td></tr>
</table>

Approaching Troops

While there still remains a chance that the approaching troops will appear on the 'enemy' base line, the likelihood of this has now been reduced.

It will doubtless be apparent to the reader that, by varying the dice scores required for certain sections of the table and indeed the actual size of those sections, the possibilities of awkward arrivals may be increased or decreased as required.

Reinforcements

The arrival and deployment of reinforcing units can clearly be treated in much the same manner. The solo player is free to weigh the odds as seen fit to suit the occasion, but perhaps the point does need to be made that reinforcements could have the advantage of 'marching to the sound of the guns' and thus reduce their chance of an unfortunate landing.

The Unpredictable Enemy

Let us assume at this stage that the terrain has been laid out for a wargame, either using one of the random selection methods suggested above or in accordance with a map. Troops have been laid out and once the non and late arrivals, defunct units etc. have been sorted out, the battle can finally commence.

There are a number of ideas and techniques which can be used to play out a solo wargame.

One system is for the solo player to identify with one army in the game and to write set orders for 'the enemy'. These may be either restrictive or have as many alternatives/options as required, decided on a 'response to own move' system or by dice throws.

Alternatively, it would be decreed that 'the enemy' can respond to situations in a fairly limited fashion. For example, it would be stipulated that line units need to score a six (Guard units five or six) on one ordinary dice in order to demonstrate any initiative in response to an attack or situation. This can be made less strict by saying that a 3–6 will permit reaction or, as always, different dice can be utilised to produce a varying range of results.

Another method altogether is to write battle plans for both armies and attempt to follow them as closely as possible. Once a decision has to be made, the solo wargamer can either come to an arbitrary result or dice for the outcome.

A third idea is to write a selection of fairly general orders, 'hold left flank, attack with right' or 'hold centre, feint with left, main thrust with right' etc., shuffle them and allot one per army. The orders can be reduced from those suitable as generalised army orders, to optional instructions applicable move by move.

Here we have come virtually full circle and are back in the realms of the chance card, with options being inserted into the game as required.

Re-Supply

The final aspect of solo play which will be discussed in this chapter is the re-supply of troops in the field. While once again arguably straying into the area already covered by chance cards, the re-supply systems here are applied rather more deliberately and steadily.

The initial and indeed the main consideration is given to ammunition. It matters little whether the ammunition in question consists of bolts for your crossbowmen or missiles for a Milan anti-tank system, the principles should remain the same.

Ordinarily, ammunition re-supply is not a factor in a wargame; time is usually too short for the consideration of such peripheral aspects. The solo player however, has all the time required and may – if so desired – consider the question fully.

The rate of fire of the weapon in question has to be calculated or estimated, based both on fact and the number of times a particular unit armed with that weapon has been in action during the game.

Here is an example. A typical French Napoleonic foot artillery battery of the line consisted of six 8pdr. cannon and a couple of 5.5in. howitzers. The chest of ammunition carried on the trail of each fieldpiece contained 15 rounds of cannon balls, the supporting ammunition wagon, or caisson as it was termed, some 62. (*Artillery Equipments Of The Napoleonic Wars*, Terence Wise, Osprey 1979). Thus each cannon had 77 rounds fairly readily available. The howitzer section of the battery was rather more complicated, but consisted mainly of fuzed shells, 49 in all. The rate of fire was standardised at one round per minute, thus the ammunition to hand would feed the gun sufficiently for just over one hour of continuous firing.

Bearing in mind that the actual rate of fire would probably have been slower – the guns are unlikely to have been in action all the time – perhaps it would be safe to permit the supply to allow two to two and a half hours' firing.

Given that the 'real' time judged to have elapsed in a wargame is usually considerably longer than this, the reader can probably appreciate that ammunition re-supply can form an interesting side issue to a solo game.

The next step would be to check the amount of ammunition

carried by the supporting artillery train column, both at battery and divisional level, and the typical deployment of these formations.

Here only one isolated example has been cited, but as previously mentioned, the principle can equally be applied to infantry (how many rounds could be carried for Spencer rifle of the American Civil War), and heavier ammunition (what was the stowage capacity for armour-piercing shells in an M4A3 HVSS Sherman tank circa 1945).

Food is more difficult to calculate and probably in all fairness comes under the broad heading of a campaign consideration, but the solo player might like to devise mechanisms based on the availability or possibly lack of food for his men.

Pay is another factor, either for one's own troops in the field or for any mercenary units. Does the army pay chest run out at the onset of the battle, causing the more fickle and greedy hired units in your army to go over to the enemy in search of a better return for their efforts?

Only the player can decide which of these additional facets he includes into the battle and to what degree they are allowed to influence its outcome. This is arguably one of the bonuses of solo play – the time to consider all aspects of a battle or campaign, either those discussed above or the dozens of others which will doubtless become apparent to the reader.

3 SMALL SCALE ACTIONS

In this chapter we will look at the smaller type of action which, although perhaps unsuitable for consideration within the context of a full scale wargame, still offers much in the way of interest for solo play.

Hopefully within the mix of both period and type of action there will be something of interest to the reader, whatever his inclination.

The situations discussed will offer ideas to be developed or perhaps new lines of thought or types of scenario. Each section can clearly be tailored to suit the individual's facilities and needs and can certainly be adapted in countless different directions.

The scenarios as described were fought with 25mm figures, but there is no reason why 15mm, 20mm, 30mm or 54mm soldiers cannot be used.

The Free Company

One of the by-products of the continuing wars between England and France in the 14th century was the emergence of bands of professional soldiers thrown into unemployment by breaks in the various campaigns. These men organised themselves into bands or 'Free Companies' and resorted to plundering villages or ransoming captives for a living. Such groups usually made a nuisance of themselves, terrorising large areas of the French countryside with their activities.

This scenario looks at an ambush situation based on a typical venture which might have been carried out by men of a Free Company.

On one side are the brigands, the number of which will depend on the resources of the player, but about a dozen should suffice. These can really be any mid-period Medieval foot soldiers, preferably with a selection of both weapons and mode of dress.

The unfortunate recipient of their attention is a nobleman,

The Boer War is an excellent period for solo wargaming. Here are two models of the protagonists in 54mm scale – a British infantryman (l) and a Boer (r).

travelling with his attendant entourage of men-at-arms, pages, squires etc., perhaps 20 figures in all, some of which are non-combatants.

The wargames table can be laid out with some fairly typical representative scenery – rocks, trees, bushes etc. and one such set-up is shown in Fig. 6.

The men of the Free Company may be placed in ambush positions or alternatively they can be represented by counters of one form or another, either on the table or on a representational map. The wargamer might like to include extra dummy counters in his deployment so that he himself is unsure as to the precise location of all the ambushers.

The travellers move along the track crossing the playing area from right to left in any sort of order deemed appropriate.

It is reasonably safe to assume that the nobleman undertaking the journey would be alive to the potential dangers involved in such a venture and would have made some preparations. These could include an advance party of mounted soldiers, flank or rear guards as well as adequate personal protection.

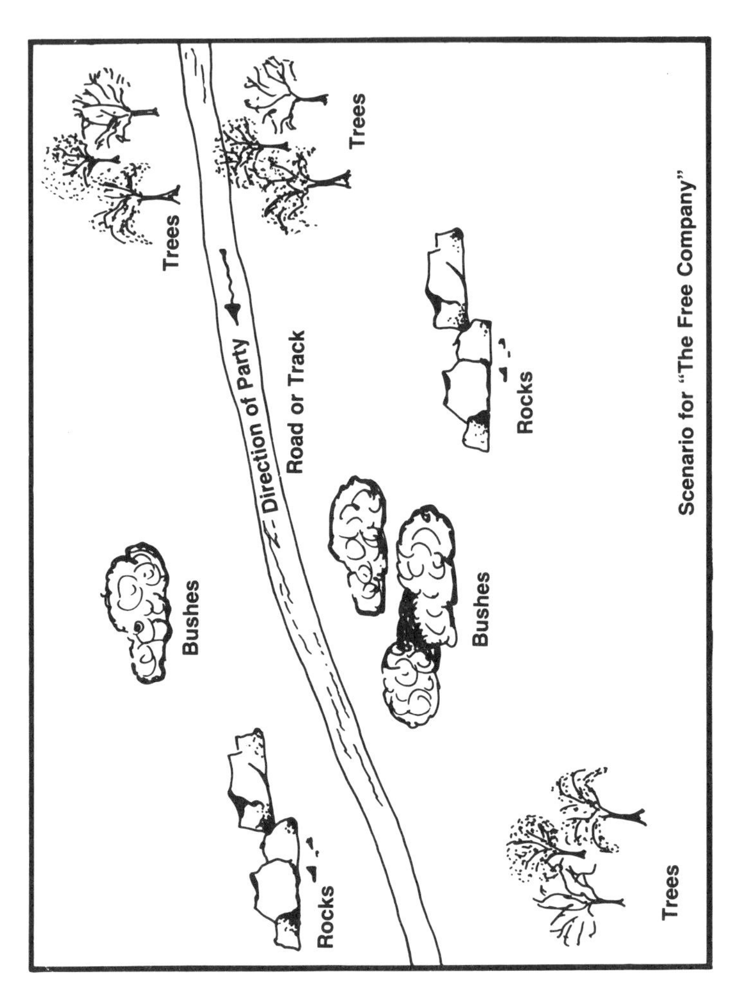

Scenario for "The Free Company"

Figure 6

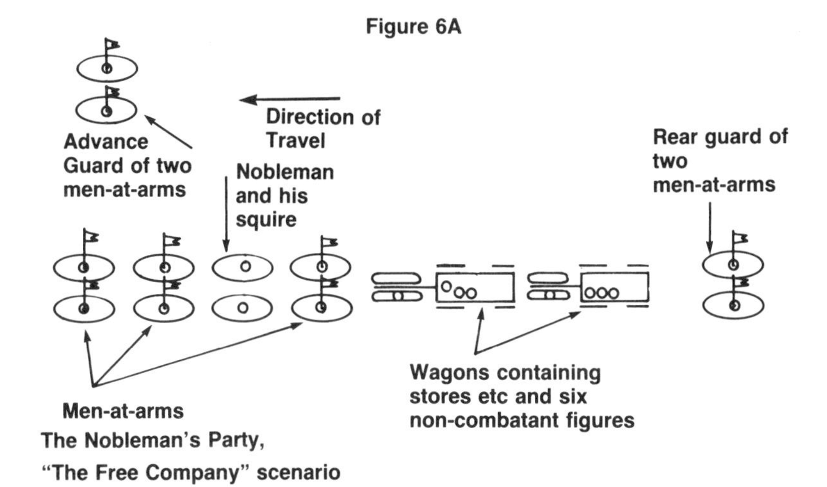

The Nobleman's Party, "The Free Company" scenario

In the sample game used to play out this particular scenario, Fig. 6A shows the formation used for the nobleman's party.

Now one of two events must take place in order for there to be a game – either the brigands successfully spring their ambush or the astute nobleman and his escort detect their presence before this occurs.

To consider the first option, the soloist can allow the nobleman's entourage to cover as much of the distance across the table as required prior to launching an attack at exactly the right moment. A rule could be introduced that the Free Company counters need dice to be thrown in order to be turned over and converted into figures. This should be fairly easy to achieve, but can include a fine degree of chance that one ambusher may not materialise to add his weight to the mêlée. One ordinary dice could be used with a score of 1–5 making each counter available and a 6 rendering a counter or man unusable.

There could be a variety of reasons for this reluctance – perhaps the opposition looks a little too well organised and, what the heck, you've done your share of risking your neck recently!

Add the two chance elements together – blank counters and reluctant heroes – and straight away the ambush party have their problems.

Unless he is a complete fool or insufferably arrogant, our nobleman – like the chap in the diagram above – will presumably have some sort of advance guard for his party. The presence of these soldiers should offer an increased chance of the ambush being detected by the travellers.

An officer and drummer of the French Imperial Guard. The Napoleonic period is rich in ideas for solo play. 25mm figures from Essex Miniatures.

A Renaissance period personality figure in 25mm scale. Such characters come into their own in solo wargames. Figure by Essex Miniatures.

A suggested rule to cover this is as follows:

At 9–12in. from the nearest ambusher, an 11 or 12 thrown on two ordinary dice will detect the presence of the trap.

At 6–9in. distance a throw of 9 or 10, again using two ordinary dice, will reveal the ambush. At 6–3in. a 7 or 8 is needed and at less than 3 inches a 5 or 6.

Thus it is by no means certain that the ambush will be detected but, the nearer the convoy gets to its site, the better their chances of doing so.

Now, the two sides in the wargame will have varying objectives. The men of the Free Company will wish to speedily despatch the men-at-arms, pages etc., but to take the nobleman alive for ransoming at a future date. The seizure of the wagons and their contents would also without doubt be viewed as a desirable bonus by them.

The nobleman and his entourage will have swift escape as their main aim, either back the way they have come or towards the table edge to which they were originally travelling.

How fervently the individual men-at-arms will defend their lord can be decided on a personalised dice score – 1 or 2 and the soldier in question worries only about himself, 3–4 and he will stay as long as the fight is going reasonably well, 5–6 and he will fight to the death to defend his lord. The non-combatants will need some slight amendment to their combat dice, a –2 on each dice thrown for them probably being sufficient to represent their lack of arms training. As always, the wargamer is free to vary the odds and required results as he wishes.

As regards the actual combat, any basic set of rules will suffice, probably the simpler the better. A straightforward dice throw can be used per combatant, highest score winning, or something slightly more sophisticated may be needed, such as a bonus of 1 on the dice rolled for a mounted man, or a +2 to that of the lord.

To represent the surprise of the ambush, the attackers could all be given a +1 or even perhaps a +2 bonus to their dice scores for the first round only. A modification of this could be that if the ambush is detected from a long distance, i.e., the 9–12in. mentioned above, then the assailants would not receive a first round bonus, at 6–9in perhaps just a +1 and so forth.

For the lord to be taken alive, a rule can be stipulated that there must be a minimum of four ambushers around him in potential mêlée positions. The lord can then 'fight' each one in turn, using a single dice roll method noted above. As soon as he loses, the lord is deemed to be captured and must be escorted by a minimum of two ambushers at all times from then on.

A command set for an 18th century action – the seizure of the colours can make an exciting solo game.

In a similar manner, the two carts can be said to be taken by the attackers if all their original occupants are either scattered or killed, and there are at least two men from the Free Company on the wagon or one of its draught animals.

In order to decide who has won the action, the convoy will have to get a certain percentage of figures or wagons to the intended table edge, or lay low a set number of their assailants. For their part, the ambushers will have to secure either the nobleman or the wagons to make their venture worthwhile.

The scenario can either be fought on a 'last man left alive' situation, or to a position where the losses of the ambushers reach a set figure – say half their total number – which will cause them to reconsider and break off the attack.

Further Reading

In order that the reader may find out more about the Free Companies, the following titles are recommended:–

Heath, I., *Armies of the Middle Ages*, Vol. I (WRG, 1982)
Wise, T., *Medieval Warfare* (Osprey, 1976)

The Indian Raid

While they were by no means the first settlers in the New World

(Jamestown, Virginia, was established in 1607), when the Pilgrim Fathers founded New Plymouth in 1620 they began the colonisation of America in the proper sense.

From the outset the settlers were destined not to find the peace and contentment they sought.

In 1626 England seized the town of New Amsterdam from the Dutch, changing its name to New York. 1635–44 saw intermittent warfare between the colonies of Maryland and Virginia while 1644–46 witnessed religious wars in the former colony, fought between Catholics and Protestants. King Philip's War 1675–76 saw England and France at odds with one another – a situation which was to last for over a century in the American colonies.

During this same period, Susquehannock Indians crossed the Potomac river eastwards into the colony of Virgina and conducted a series of raids against the settlers there. It is one of these raids, or rather its wargame creation, that will form the basis of the next minor action.

The setting is a group of timber huts or small houses, complete with an encircling stockade and watchtower. The occupants – colonists, pioneers, settlers, call them what you will – are hardy folk, used to fighting for what they want. The early occupants of such townships were citizen soldiers who developed their own militia companies. While such companies initially consisted of one-third pike and two-thirds muskets, the pike quickly fell into disuse and all the men became musket-armed. The wooden building can be improvised, scratchbuilt or culled from a variety of sources. (Check out the inexpensive self-assembly, pre-coloured card village sets from *Games Workshop*, for example.)

The wooden stockade and watch tower – which, if desired, can be classed as an optional extra – can similarly be improvised.

A good deal of peripheral greenery is needed for effect and setting but, since areas around settlements were usually cleared of trees and undergrowth, no fighting need take place amongst the trees, lichen etc.

A suggested layout is sketched in Fig. 7.

Finally, the figures. English Civil War musketeers are eminently suitable for portraying the colonists, while the Indians can be represented by virtually any suitable figure. Several manufacturers of wargame figures produce American Civil War, American War of Independence, Seven Years War or US Indian War ranges and each features, or rather should feature, several Indian types which can be utilised for the present scenario. My own Indian figures are the plastic variety marketed by Spencer-

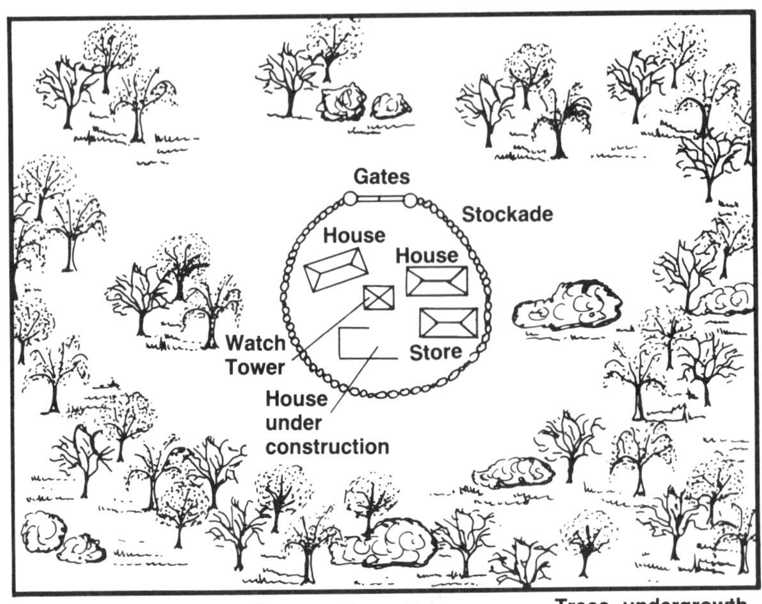

"The Indian Raid" scenario Figure 7 Trees, undergrowth etc all around stockade

Smith and have seen service in many campaigns and actions set in the 18th and 19th centuries. The 'settlers' for their part last saw action on Naseby field, but seem to have survived their 65 day Atlantic crossing and thirty-year time shift well enough!

There are several ways in which the solo player can handle this scenario.

One option is for the soloist to take the side of the Susquehannocks. This means that the settlers will have fixed roles and reactions, governed by dice or chance cards or even, perhaps, lacking variables entirely. If, for example, we state that there are to be 12 able-bodied colonists on the stockade – this seems a fair number, but can of course be varied as required – then it seems not unreasonable to stipulate that in such a hostile environment, two of their number will be on watch at any given time.

In the diagram, the watch tower has been placed among the houses but it could equally well form an integral part of the surrounding stockade.

One of the colonists would be in the tower, presumably, and another perhaps by the gates. Should either of the sentries detect movement, noise or whatever, then they will quickly raise the

Frei Korps 15 Apache Indians in 15mm scale, useful for Indian raid scenarios.

alarm and call their colleagues to arms – shall we give them a 6in. move?

Thus the solo player can allot set positions to the two sentries and establish reaction times for the other occupants of the stockade. Perhaps a dice can be thrown for each figure, offering some delay in response, but in all fairness the odds should be in favour of the defenders reacting fairly speedily to any alarm call.

Since the settlers are in a confined area and can only respond to an attack, the solo player wishing to play the role of Indian commander (or should that be Indian chief?) can have a fairly free hand to place his men wherever is seen fit. The Indians – 20 figures perhaps – can creep up on the stockade with only a slight chance of detection for, after all, they were past masters at hunting and tracking.

For this section of the scenario, it may be opportune to use two percentage dice and stipulate that only a throw of 90–99% will alert the sentries to the presence of the Indians, for as long as the warriors remain outside the stockade.

Once a feathered head pops over the wall, however, the sentry must have a much better chance of spotting it and the player can then use the outcome of a six-sided dice roll, heavily weighted in favour of the colonists.

Once detected, there may be time for some firing – the muskets in use would be of the matchlock type and thus have a slow rate of fire – before hand-to-hand combat. The Indian speed of movement should be faster than that of the defenders, so they can cover 9in. per move.

As soon as the mêlée ensues then any identity the player may have with the Indians will be lost as numerous combats will need to be sorted.

Let us leave it there for the moment and this time let the solo

Figures from RAFM which are ideal for 25mm solo skirmish games set in 18th century North America.

player take control of the defenders rather than the Susquehannock attackers. To simulate the surprise appearance of the Indians on the walls it is suggested that the soloist regards the stockade as a clockface. Two ordinary dice are thrown for each warrior who is then placed at the appropriate place outside the stockade.

In Figure 7 the gates – a suitable reference point – could be considered as being 12 o'clock, a point directly opposite and across the settlement 6 o'clock and so on. Thus all the Indians can be sited on a random basis. The next step is for the attack to start at each brave attempt to cross the wall. Using one ordinary dice this time, it could be said that 1–2 and he slips over undetected, but 3–6 he is spotted and the alarm raised.

So using some fairly simple mechanisms the solo player can, if required, identify with either, both or neither sides in this particular scenario.

Once the firing and mêlée have broken out any set of period rules will suffice to cover the situation, but once again probably the simpler the better, bearing in mind the soloist is now controlling perhaps over 30 figures.

Combats could either be on a single dice roll – one per figure, highest wins – or in a more sophisticated skirmish, wargame style, depending on the needs and preferences of the individual wargamer.

The Susquehannocks could perhaps be given a +1 to the first roll only of their dice when they mêlée one of the first settlers who is just stumbling out of one of the houses.

If it is desired, the warriors could be given bows and arrows and thus enjoy a much higher rate of fire than the musket armed settlers. Given a 12in. range for the bow a 6 on one ordinary dice could kill at 9–12in. range, 4–6 at 3–6in. range and perhaps 2–6 at 0–3in. distance, firing twice per move. So that our warriors do not become supermen, if they fire once their normal 9in. move is reduced to 6in., fire twice and they move only 3in. The musket is less reliable and it is suggested that at the three range bands just quoted a 6, 5–6 and 4–6 would be suitable requirements for a target to be hit; the musket will fire once every other move, needing a full and uninterrupted move between firings to facilitate re-loading. The solo player will probably need to keep a close check on the status of his 12 settlers' muskets as the scenario unfolds.

To win the game, the Indians have to despatch the settlers and perhaps seize some form of plunder. This latter can have a stylised representation in the form of a number of sacks or barrels, stored in each house (physically or on paper). One brave is

The US cavalry fought a long series of wars against the American Indians in the 19th century. The 54mm figure is very suitable for the recreation of such actions.

available to carry one sack or barrel with a one third reduction in his speed. Such items can be thrown over the stockade and collected on the far side. The marauders' morale must be suspect, however, and a rule could be introduced that once they lose a third of their number the Indians will break off the attack and high-tail it back to the woods. If one third is deemed too severe then one half can be adopted, or whatever proportion seems applicable to the player.

For the defenders to win they have only to drive off their attackers and preserve their stores.

For further information on this period the wargamer is recommended to read:–

Dupuy, R. & T., *The Encyclopedia of Military History* (Macdonald, 1970)

Funcken, L. & F., *L'Uniforme et Les Armes des Soldats des Etats-Unis* (2 vols) (Casterman, 1979)

Russia 1812

The retreat from Moscow by the French Grande Armee in the latter months of 1812 is a well-documented affair, but we can still only imagine the cold, deprivation and hunger suffered by the soldiers as they trudged ever westwards. As if this were not sufficient, the troops were continually harassed by Russian irregular light cavalrymen – the Cossacks.

Mounted on sturdy ponies, these men were able to live off the inhospitable land and were employed by the Russian army not for pay but for plunder.

This scenario portrays the progress of a section of French infantrymen in the face of the unforgiving elements and the relentless Cossacks.

The playing area can be laid as shown in Fig. 8. The use of a white tablecloth or sheet as a covering for the playing area offers a simple and speedy method of portraying the snow-covered terrain of Russia.

There is no track or path across the playing area, but the group of French soldiers are attempting to cross from right to left in as much of a straight line as they can.

The Cossacks for their part are determined both to prevent this and to reduce the numbers of the retreating group.

The French can cover 6in. per move, but after three moves of continuous movement or action, must spend one complete turn without moving or firing. This stricture is designed to reflect the

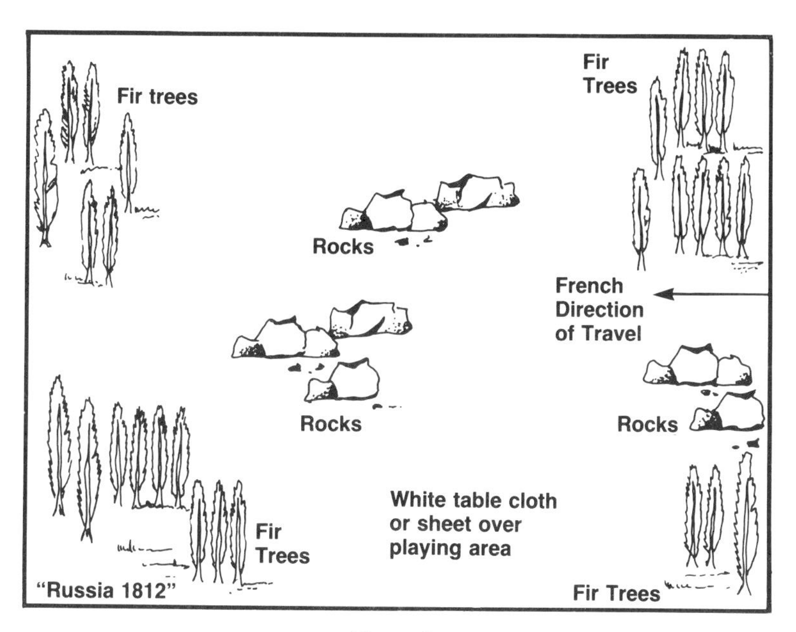

Figure 8

Great-coated French infantry close ranks in order to fend off some marauding Russian cossacks.

tiredness of the men, but variations can be introduced to ensure that the halts thus imposed are not too regular.

As regards numbers, 12–15 French sounds about right with perhaps the same number of Cossacks.

All the French can have muskets, or if it is felt more representative, a certain number may have to make do with either mêlée weapons – swords, halberds and the like – or improvised weapons such as clubs. A dice roll can set the numbers of each type if required.

It seems likely that due to both the conditions and fatigue the soldiers will be much slower to load their muskets and thus should perhaps only be able to fire every other move. Maybe a limit on their ammunition could be imposed, but this may be deemed a little too harsh.

The accuracy of the French firing could be questionable due again to the situation and the swift-moving Cossack targets. At 0–6in. a 5 or 6 on one dice is required to kill one Russian, at 6–12in. only a 6 will empty the saddle.

The Cossacks are all mounted and may move 12in. per move. They are armed only with mêlée weapons – lance and sword and thus must close to contact with the French to kill. In mêlée, however, the Cossacks have the benefit of +1 to their dice to represent their advantage in being mounted.

Russian Cossacks, the much feared light cavalry of the Steppes. These are converted Spencer-Smith 30mm plastic figures.

Additional ideas can be incorporated if required – for example the French could be penalised if they halt for more than, say, two consecutive moves. When this happens each man could have two ordinary dice rolled for him with a double meaning that he has finally succumbed to the conditions and his figure is then removed.

It is unlikely the Cossacks will cease harrying the party, but a rule could be stipulated that once they lose half their number they will withdraw two full moves and spend the next move considering their position very carefully.

Thus the scenario should form the basis of an interesting game, the slower-moving French with a degree of firepower against the faster-moving Russians with none at all.

The solo player can equally easily identify with one side or the other or control the entire game as so few figures are involved.

Taking the Fort

The inspiration for this particular scenario came from the taking of the Taku forts in China in 1860.

In days of playing with toy soldiers prior to proper wargaming being discovered, many of my battles revolved around toy forts of one style or another. Oddly enough, however, very few wargames feature such items, which is, on reflection, a curious state of affairs.

In an attempt to rectify this, a situation involving a fort was deemed proper and the US Cavalry/Indian or Foreign Legion/Arab scenarios sprang to mind.

During the course of research, however, one particular action against a fort, or rather forts, came to light. In 1860 British troops stormed the Taku forts, strongholds held by the Chinese, thus offering a rather unusual twist – the irregulars were on the inside and the regular troops undertaking the assault. It is from this incident that this scenario draws much of its inspiration.

The general layout may be seen in Fig. 9.

The fort in use is the old Airfix 'Fort Sahara' which has seen many battles, set in many periods. If this particular piece does not number amongst the soloist's terrain items a similar structure is easy enough to scratchbuild. Really, the fort should be of the 'hardened mud' variety rather than of stone in order to better reflect the original situation, but this requirement is not of paramount importance. Provided there is room for the defenders to move around inside the fort, its walls are not too high and it does not cover too much of the playing area, all will be well.

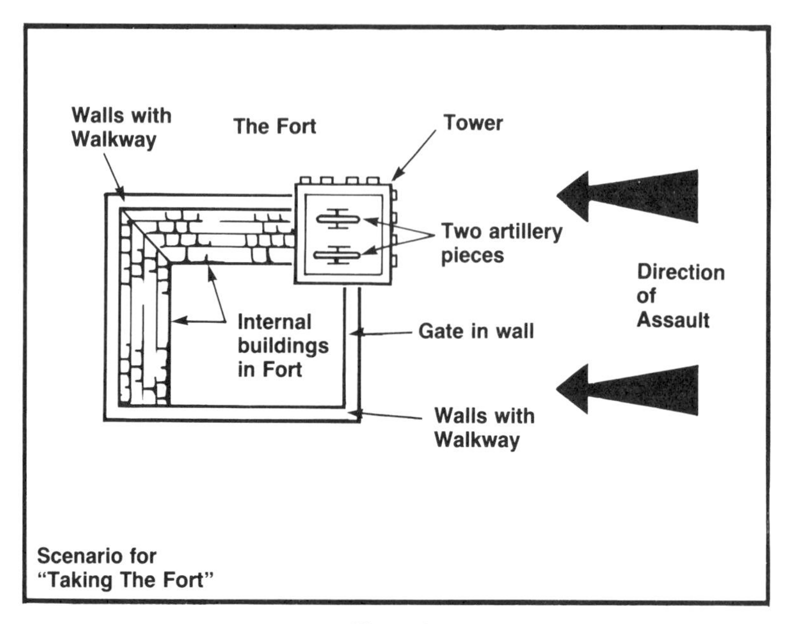

Figure 9

The defenders in this scenario were provided by the Chinese figures in the 'Red Wing' range of Boxer Rebellion figures, the attackers by suitably painted (as British) ESCI Foreign Legionnaires.

This scenario takes the form of an attack on a strongpoint rather than that of a last stand. Given suitable gains by the attackers, the defenders will break and run.

To examine the defenders first. One of the limits on their number will be the physical size of the fort itself, allied to the total figures the soloist wishes to control. Between 20 and 30 would seem to satisfy both criteria, but needless to say this can be altered to suit local needs. The original Taku forts boasted a fair amount of artillery which was represented in the wargame by the addition of two garrison-mounted cannon to the fort, the crews being drawn from the already allotted garrison strength.

The attackers should outnumber the defenders by quite reasonable odds in the order of 1:3 or perhaps 1:4. This may tax both resources and playability and so once again may be varied to suit local conditions.

While the original attackers may have had the benefit of

supporting artillery, those in the scenario do not. Their only means of entry is by scaling ladders, of which there is an unlimited supply.

And so to the rules. Movement for both sides can be 6in. per side with a reduction of 3in. if the figure fires. Two attackers are needed to carry a scaling ladder and they move at 4in. per move when doing so. If one figure is killed, either the movement of the ladder stops until another figure arrives or one man may carry the ladder at 2in. per move. If a new man arrives to carry the ladder in place of a casualty then the ladder may be moved in accordance with the amount of move distance the new arrival has left, to a maximum of 4in., and there is no penalty for him picking the ladder up.

To place the ladder against the walls of the fort takes 2in. of a move and requires two men to carry out the act. An unoccupied ladder may be cast down by the defenders with a throw of 5 or 6 on one ordinary dice, but there is no limit to the number of times a ladder can be cast down or replaced.

The attackers move up the ladder in one move and the leading man may fight a mêlée in that same move. If he is killed the defender may throw down the ladder with a score of 6 on one ordinary dice. The other men on the ladder have to be diced for individually: a 1 or 2 and they are deemed casualties and removed.

Mêlées are decided on a highest dice wins basis, with one ordinary dice being thrown for each figure. The defender has the benefit of a +1 on his mêlée all the time he is on the wall and the attacker is on the ladder. Should the attacker win the mêlée he can occupy the defender's place on the wall, but may then have to face several defenders at once. This situation is resolved by allowing the attacker to take on each defender in turn. Thus he may either lay low one or several of his assailants, or alternatively last only a short time on the wall. Should he meet his end, his ladder cannot be thrown down, for there will be another attacker at its top (unless the assaulters are running low on men) who will have to be tested before an attempt can be made.

Once the attackers establish a foothold on the walls, men can climb over to support them at the rate of two figures per move, always assuming there are sufficient numbers available.

The defenders do have some fire power and it may be as well to consider this aspect here. Firstly the artillery, though this is really only of use during the initial charge against the walls. The initial start line for the attackers should be perhaps three or four moves

A striking view of the detailed interior of an Afghan hill fort by Ian Weekley of Battlements. As the centre piece of a wargame, such forts are extremely useful.

away from the fort, so it is probably not unreasonable to stipulate that they are under fire from the word go. If we allow our garrison artillery a range of 24in. with half an ordinary dice throw for effect at over 12in. and a full one at less than that distance, we shall not be too far out.

To simulate the small arms fire of the defenders – the percentage of their numbers so equipped may be diced for – a 12in. range will suffice. At 0–6in. a 5 or 6 will kill one figure, 6–12in. a 6 is required. Clearly there can be no firing into a mêlée for there is an equal chance of a defender being killed by such an incautious shot.

Losses will probably decide the outcome of this scenario with an acceptable figure being pre-determined. One aspect the solo player might like to consider is the point that the defenders may have a degree of fanaticism about them. This was certainly the case with the Taku fort action where the defenders clung on long after one could have expected them to surrender.

Thus the attackers could call off the assault if their numbers fall to say a half, but an optional rule could be introduced to permit the defenders' numbers to drop to as low as a third before they have to give in.

There is little point in the player identifying with either side in this scenario. Many small combats and deeds of derring-do will combine to produce a most stimulating action from which the solo wargamer can reap much enjoyment. Numerous variations on a theme will readily occur to the soloist.

Perhaps the first member of the attacking forces to tear down the defenders' flag receives an instant commission or advancement. Equally the first man across the wall could be promoted and hopefully live to enjoy the benefits.

As always the player is free to alter and amend as required.

Francs-Tireurs

During the Franco-Prussian War 1870–71, local companies of irregular, largely undisciplined citizen soldiers or Francs-Tireurs were raised by the French. These companies, which had many foreign sympathisers in their ranks, operated with increasing boldness as the war progressed. The communications of the invading Prussian armies were constantly harassed by these auxiliary forces, the rail network being a popular target.

While the Francs-Tireurs could, and indeed did, operate in conjunction with regular French troops, it is their ability to disrupt the Prussian communications that forms the basis of this particular scenario.

The setting is an attack by a unit of the Francs-Tireurs; the size of the unit can be varied to suit local needs, but generally between 12 and 20 figures will be found to be suitable.

To oppose the Frenchmen, a unit of Bavarian infantry has been detailed to hold the goods depot shed which is situated by a junction in the railway lines.

Again numbers can be varied but the German strength should be between half and two thirds that of their attackers.

The French aim is to destroy the railway points, thus rendering the track unusable, while the Bavarians are there to prevent just such an occurrence.

The playing area may be set out as in Fig. 10.

The depot shed is a quite large if somewhat ruinous affair and for the purpose of the wargame it may be found to be advantageous if it has a removable roof.

The linesmen's huts are no more than shanties in some degree of dilapidation and the disused coal stores are open-topped, three sided affairs built from old railway sleepers.

All these items, including railway track itself, needless to say, can be either scratchbuilt or obtained from a reasonably equipped hobby or model railway shop.

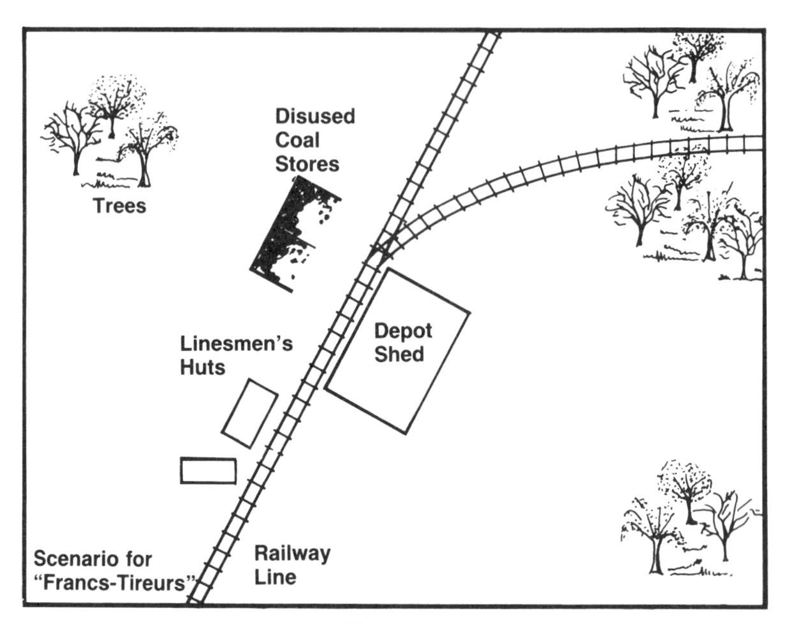

Figure 10

The figures used in the play testing of this scenario were all by Wargames Foundry, who offer an excellent range of high quality 25mm figures for the period. Any suitable troops will suffice, however, notably American Civil War Federal infantry, who will serve equally well either as Francs-Tireurs or kepi-clad German Wurttemberg infantry to defend the depot. At a pinch Napoleonic Bavarians will serve as their fellow-countrymen some 60 years later, but the ACW figures as Wurttembergers are a better bet.

Only two general rules are needed for this particular scenario – movement and firing. The first one is quickly settled, 6in. per figure per move being quite reasonable, with no deduction for firing. The rules to govern the firing of the figures are less easy to legislate. The French rifle was better than that of the Prussians, both in terms of range and rate of fire.

Admittedly the Francs-Tireurs were not first class line troops, but that does not necessarily mean that they were poor shots as a result. Equally, the military value of Prussia's southern allies, which included Bavaria and Wurttemberg, was held in question by the Prussians themselves.

To reflect the relative indiscipline of the French, the superior rate of fire of their Chassepot rifles has been ignored for the purposes of this action. The extra range, however, has been retained and the following firing rules result:

Firing (one ordinary dice per figure)

Francs-Tireurs	Bavarian
0–6in. 4, 5, 6 to kill 1 figure	0–6in. 4, 5, 6 to kill 1 figure
6–12in. 5, 6	6–12in. 5, 6
12–18in. 6	

It is unlikely that the Germans guarding the rail junction will be on full alert, so one sentry has been posted outside the depot shed and the rest of their number is inside the building.

Here the solo player can decide which side is to be played and which to be 'regulated', or both sides can be controlled if required.

Let us consider playing the French first. With the German sentry in place, the rest of the guard need a response time once alerted. There will be no need for them to leave the shed – they will adopt firing positions from within. It will probably be sufficient merely to bar the Bavarians from firing in the move immediately after the one in which the alarm is raised. After this they can move and fire as required, but once firing positions have been adopted, there is

Bavarian infantry move to defend the railway line against the French irregulars.

little chance of movement, thus making the Germans ideal as a 'regulated' enemy.

The French can advance from any direction either on a random or selective basis. The whole purpose of their mission is to jam the railway points, remember, and to achieve this two of their number must be in contact with the points for two subsequent uninterrupted moves and may perform no other action.

For the Bavarians to be 'played', random or again selective, entry and movement for the French can be determined by dice scores, as can their success or failure at jamming the railway points.

The dubious cover afforded to the defenders by the shed is countered by the fact that the Francs-Tireurs have the option to adopt the prone position. While they may fire lying down, they cannot move, so any benefit to each side is cancelled out and therefore there is no reduction for targets under cover.

The scenario will doubtless run as a prolonged fire-fight, so the soloist may require a morale rule to evoke when either side's losses reach a pre-determined number or percentage. At what level this is set depends on the player's requirements and to a lesser extent on the number of figures involved.

A 'fight to the finish' in the style of H.G. Wells can result if required, either side can be reduced to say half strength and then retire hastily.

The zest and relative inefficiency of both sides can be reflected and countered if required. The elan of irregular Francs-Tireurs may dissipate under fire from regular troops and the attack – probably largely un-coordinated – falter. Equally the relative professionalism of the Bavarians may thin under impetuous attack, making even the hostile French countryside seem that bit more inviting.

The scenarios may only have two main results – either the French jam the points or they do not – but there can be many twists along the way.

Further reading

Howard, M., *The Franco-Prussian War* (Methuen, 1985)

May, R. & Embleton, G., *The Franco Prussian War 1870* (Almark, 1975)

4 HISTORICAL SOLO PLAY

In this section of the book two larger battles are considered in the light of their potential as solo wargames. The main purpose is to allow the solo player to operate or control one army while the opposition follows set orders or manoeuvres.

One of the easiest ways to achieve this is to place 'the opposition' in a defensive position and then for the solo player to carry out attacks on this position.

A couple of battles which lend themselves to this style of action are discussed below, but without doubt the reader will be aware of many more actions which are equally suitable.

Borodino 1812

The battle of Borodino, fought on September 7th 1812, was the largest action brought about by Napoleon's invasion of Russia with his Grande Armee.

After continually giving ground, the Russian commander-in-chief General Kutusov adopted a firm defensive position against the French in and to the south of Borodino village. There were in fact two Russian armies present at the battle, namely the First and Second Armies of the West. In all the Russian commander had 120,000 troops supported by 640 pieces of artillery at his disposal as he organised his deployment.

The key points of the Russian line are sketched out in Fig. 11.

The amount of detail which the wargamer wishes to incorporate into the construction and laying out of the terrain is up to the individual. The villages and earthworks can be built as fully detailed replicas or merely basic outlines of the original. None of the items are over-difficult to produce, however, and all are available as commercial items in several scales. Generally speaking it is true to say that the better the terrain the better the game, but if the wargamer is using, say, counters for figures, then the terrain to a certain extent is of lesser importance.

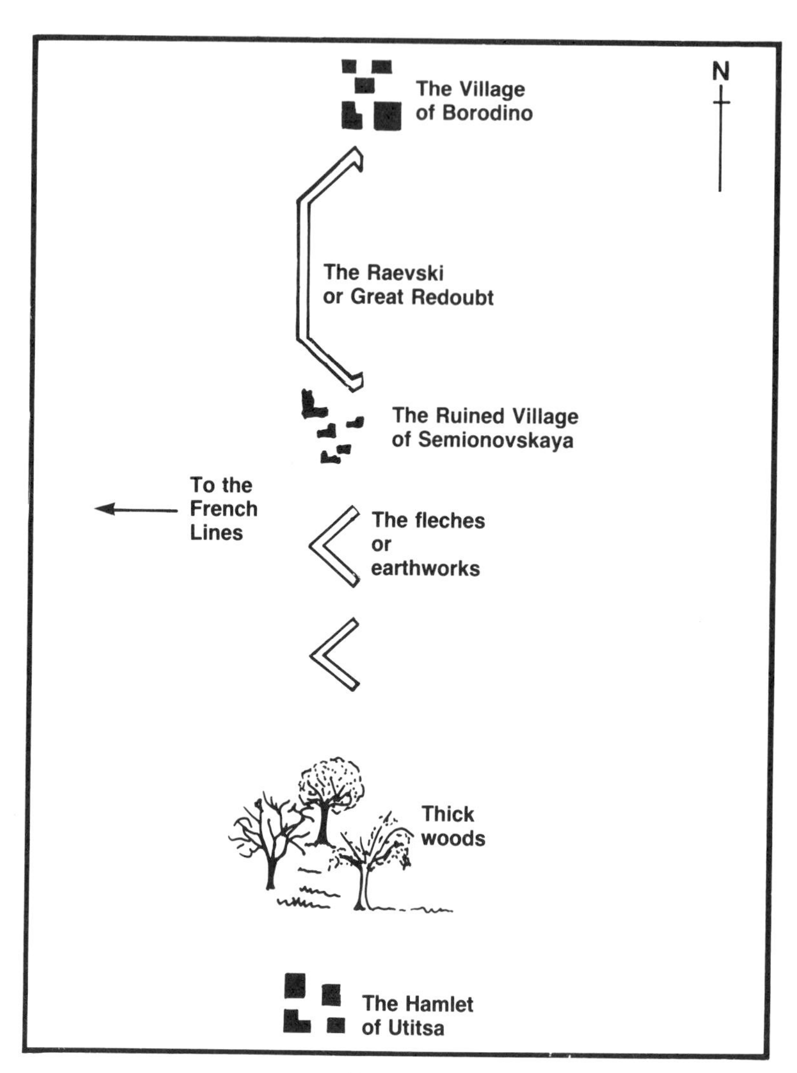

Figure 11

The key points in the Russian defensive line at Borodino 1812

The actual deployment achieved by the Russians will largely depend on the number of figures available to the solo player. For the purposes of the game the defending soldiers do not all have to be Russian – other suitable figures can be pressed into service – although this may be deemed to be aesthetically unpleasing. Borodino was a large action, however, and 120,000 soldiers take a lot of representing on the table top. Even if using fairly large ratio of one wargames figure purporting to represent 100 actual men, 1,200 such figures will be needed. Move up to an even larger ratio, say 1:1000, and only 120 figures will be needed, but this number of soldiers at once becomes totally unconvincing as the forces required for a large battle.

There are a few alternative solutions that can be offered. Firstly smaller figures can be used, such as 6mm troop blocks. These little figures occupy very little space on the wargames table, are fairly quick to paint and offer the chance of using a much smaller figure/man ratio. All these advantages are the reasons behind the introduction of such blocks, which continue to increase in popularity with wargamers.

Instead of the troop block concept, formations of 6mm figures can be organised using single castings and once again the resultant units occupy very little space – the proverbial army in a cigar box.

Clearly it is more appealing if both sides are fully represented by hordes of miniature soldiery in 6,15, 20 or 25mm, but the action is not insoluble if the soloist lacks troops in sufficient numbers. For the solo wargamer it is the involvement that is the main contributing factor to the enjoyment of the hobby.

Cardboard counters – either home made or temporarily borrowed from a suitable board game – can be utilised. To scratchbuild (if that is the correct expression in this context) the counters is an attractive concept, for it means that each of the contending armies can be fairly easily recreated in their entirety

15mm Prussian and Russian Napoleonics from Frei Korps 15. Using these smaller figures, the wargamer can field larger armies.

down to whatever organisational level the soloist deems both appropriate and manageable.

The battle can be fought using such counters on either the table top or on a map, be it home produced or a commercial product. It is feasible, also, that just the defenders could be signified by counters, while the attacking forces are represented by wargames figures. The concept of soldiers assaulting positions manned by squares of card takes a little getting used to, but can be quite a viable proposition.

Finally the defending forces have perhaps the ultimate option – they do not have to be represented at all! Providing the attackers follow faithfully the phases of the action, then the defenders' responses and initiatives can be reacted to without them ever being carried out.

Borodino has been selected as a suitable early 19th century subject for solo play chiefly because of the defensive nature of the Russian forces in the battle. They held the line, gave some ground, put in localised counter attacks and finally all the army retired eastwards to the next ridge. It is suggested that it is not inconceivable to carry out these manoeuvres without the physical presence of wargames figures.

Whatever method is used to represent the defending Russian forces, their initial deployment and subsequent actions are the key factors in the representation of the Battle of Borodino as a solo wargame. While fairly accurate maps and diagrams of Kutusov's actual deployments can be studied in the various works on the battle, much will depend on how many Russian figures the wargamer has available. Provided that the six main strong points are defended and that some reserves are retained behind the main line, all should be well.

The French for their part had 133,000 men and 587 pieces of artillery, so whatever system was used, the same should be employed for the French.

The main phases of the battle can be summarised as follows:

1. Main French attack on the Russian left.
2. The French take the village of Borodino.
3. French also take the hamlet of Utitsa and penetrate into the area south of Semionovskaya.

So far, all goes well for the French assault, but then the Russian defenders begin to counter the French attacks.

4. The French having taken Borodino are checked by the Great Redoubt.
5. The French attack to the north of the just-taken Uititsa peters out and the attack on Semionovskya is countered by the Russians.

The French bolster up their assault:

6. The French effort against Semionovskaya is strenghtened but to no avail, so more troops are brought in.
7. The Fleches fall into French hands
   The Russians respond with increased counter-attacks.
8. Russians attack Borodino, the French hold but their intended attack on the Great Redoubt is deferred.
9. The French attack in the Utitsa area becomes bogged down.
10. The Russian lines hold against a large French cavalry attack.

Finally, the Russian lines give:

11. A Russian counter attack on Semionovskaya is halted by the French reserve artillery.
12. Utitsa is retaken and held by the French.
13. The French are now in possession of all the original Russian line positions.

Anywhere else but Russia and this would have been a victory to the French – in fact, some sources claim it to be so – but all that happened was that Kutusov's men retired back to the next ridge and formed a new line.

Overnight, however, the Russians did decide to call it a day and retreated eastwards, leaving the French in possession of the field, thus giving some credence to their claim of a victory.

From this brief summary of the battle's main components it can be seen that sections 4, 5, 6, 8, 9, 10 and 11 can be programmed actions by the defenders. Now, the attacking army cannot make war by timetable perhaps, but the defenders can! Those six sections can each be set to take place at a given stage of the battle, leaving the attacker to work out the response.

It is up to the individual player just how many variables are inserted into these responses. Too many alternatives and it is not Borodino that is being refought, but a Napoleonic defensive battle. Too few and the wargamer will be able to calculate precisely at what moment each phase will start and end. Either is enjoyable and it is entirely at the whim of the soloist as to what happens.

Each of the identified phases may be altered or played through as required. To take phase 1 as an example – the French attack on the Russian left can be successful, thrown back or brought to a halt. To follow the battle, the first outcome should occur, but the remaining two can offer some stimulating problems and situations.

Much depends on the degree of flexibility the solo player wishes the defenders to enjoy. They can be made to follow exactly the pattern set by their historical forebears or can enjoy the undoubted benefits of hindsight. The solo player is free to follow history or to try out new angles of approach and changes in strategy. Perhaps the most satisfying method is to play the battle 'straight' and then to re-run the action incorporating the required number of variants. If desired, each phase of the battle can be explored in detail, each forming an interesting action in its own right – 13 wargames in one, no less!

While many variables are feasible it is suggested that the wargamer continues to identify with the attacking army, leaving the defenders to initiate or respond by programme as required.

To wargame a Napoleonic action such as Borodino in a manner that is as historically accurate as possible is a very stimulating affair. Rules, drawn up to cover that one specific battle, can reflect the tactics of the day without the usual attendant problems of the generalisation made necessary by wider coverage of period.

As has been noted previously time is a great asset of the solo player – time to ponder a point, to re-play a section of the battle, time to stop and check a reference or two, time to jot down the odd comment or rule suggestion. Such actions would doubtless drive a 'live' opponent wild, but to the soloist they are part and parcel of the immense enjoyment and involvement that can be derived from the hobby by such an approach. To see an actual battle unfold on one's table top is fascinating and carrying out 'what if' exercises based on that battle is a totally absorbing pastime.

Suvla Bay 1915

For our second larger battle we move on just over a century to the Great War.

The Allied attack against the Gallipoli peninsula was designed to defeat the Turkish army, thereby causing her ally Germany to detach men from the deadlocked Western Front in order to support her. This would then tip the manpower balance in favour of the Allies and increase the chance of that ever-elusive break-through taking place.

So much for the strategy, which was both bold and imaginative. The reality however was a different story. The Allies landed 70,000 men, of whom a fair proportion were from the Australian and New Zealand Army Corps (ANZAC). Immediately after landing the British and Commonwealth troops were pinned down on the beaches and could make little or no progress inland. Under constant and accurate fire from the Turkish soldiers positioned on the heights which dominated the beaches, the Allies began to suffer heavy casualties and frustration set in.

The Allied commander, Lt.-General Sir Ian Hamilton, conceived the plan to land troops to the north of his beleaguered ANZACS and ease the pressure on them. Accordingly IX Corps of the Allied army – some 22 infantry battalions – under the command of Lt.-General Stopford landed at Suvla Bay. Unfortunately the newly arrived troops did not immediately make for the dominant ridges to support their comrades to the south, but remained in the vicinity of the shoreline. General Stopford was relieved of his command, but the moment had passed, for the Turks had now reinforced the ridge line.

Thus the second landing fared no better than the first and the eventual outcome was the evacuation of all the Allied forces from the peninsula in January 1916. The result ensured that the Western Front was committed to trench warfare for a further two years.

Clearly, from the Turkish point of view Suvla Bay – and indeed for that matter the entire Gallipoli affair – was a text-book defensive battle. From their strong positions a mere two kilometres inland, the well-entrenched Turkish soldiers were able to bring continuous and accurate fire down onto the stranded Allies.

It may already be apparent to the reader that when recreating this battle the actual physical presence of the Turkish forces is unnecessary on the wargames table.

To what extent the Allied forces are represented will to a large degree depend on the resources of the wargamer.

A full blown re-fight of Suvla Bay could involve the use of landing ships and armoured barges as the troops actually came ashore. This could be a fascinating aspect to wargame, but probably limits the scale of figures used to 6mm, due to the sheer scope of the landings.

Alternatively, the presence of the ships could simply be assumed with the troops starting from the water line, i.e. the table or playing area edge.

The speed of movement inland for the attackers should be fairly slow, since the entire area was swept by rifle and artillery fire. Much will depend on the scale of the figures in use – 15, 20 or 25mm, but certainly no more than say 2in. per move should be allowed. Here we are assuming all infantrymen, for armour and cavalry played no part in this action.

The Allies did have some artillery support, but there seems little point in concocting complicated rules for its movement and deployment. The prolific 5in. howitzer, for example, had a range of some six miles, so that anything on the table is potentially within range – assuming a clear line of sight – so there is little to be gained from advancing one's Allied artillery. Once a good firing site has been located, the guns can be deployed and left to get on with the business of firing.

Thus the movement for the Allies is a simple affair – or is it? If it was merely a question of marching up from the beach to the hill line, then that would have been no problem. The whole area, however, was under heavy fire, making any movement difficult. The disruptive effect of shellfire should be reflected by causing erratic progress on the attackers.

There are a number of ways of achieving this on the wargames table. If a unit – and this can be taken to mean one of any size as required – comes under fire, then it must immediately lie down, thereby rendering movement difficult. The troops can still crawl forwards, but at only ½in. per move.

For the purposes of definition 'under fire' can be taken as meaning shells landing within 6in. of a unit. In cases of contention, always measure to the centre of any formation which is under fire. Thus if a particular unit is under continuous bombardment – a highly likely event – then its movement will be restricted.

Small arms fire can still take place whatever rate of movement is achieved. As with artillery fire, range is not a problem, but hitting the target certainly is. It is suggested that two percentage dice are used to assess the effectiveness of the Allies' rifle fire against the well positioned Turks, with only a score of 90–99% being sufficient to register a hit.

Two dice can be thrown for each figure firing or if this is found to be too repetitive, some shorthand method could be used to represent the fire of an infantry unit – squad, platoon or company etc. as required. For example, assume for a moment that we are using a figure scale of 1:25, then six wargame figures would represent an infantry company of 150 men. Given a rate of rifle fire of perhaps ten rounds per minute, much will then depend on the amount of time the wargame move is taken as representing. To continue our example, assume the convenient one minute move is utilised, thus we have 60 wargame shots to consider, representing perhaps 1,500 actual ones. Here the two percentage dice could be rolled for every 10 wargame shots or for the whole 60. Granted the effect would have to be considered in the same terms – one 'hit' lays low 25 of the enemy and two hits 50 etc., but that represents only minimal bookwork. There need be no saving throws for the Turkish defenders for they already have been given an 80% chance of surviving.

The Turkish rifle fire can be represented in the same manner, but it is suggested that due to their superior position, they achieve a hit with 70% and over, again using two percentage dice.

This leaves the question of artillery fire. The best idea may be to assume that all 'guns' are in fact howitzers firing high explosive shells. Such ammunition used impact blast as well as fragmentation and some shells had a fuse that delayed their explosion, while others burst overhead.

To consider the fire of the defenders: it is virtually certain that they would have ranges down onto the beaches calculated and set to a fine degree. One method of simulating this fact is to divide the Allied part of the wargames table into square or oblong areas or 'fire zones'. This is best done on a sketch map of the battlefield rather than on the tabletop itself. Within the fire zones, the Turkish fire can be considered as methodical or random. To achieve this the fire zones can themselves be sub-divided into ten or twelve 'shell squares' as shown in Fig. 12.

If it is felt by the wargamer that the defender's fire is best represented by methodical fire, squares 1–4 are hit in sequence, then 5–8, then 9–12. Once the cycle is complete, square 1 is fired on and the whole thing begins again. If a random method is used then two ordinary dice are utilised, their combined score indicating which square has been hit. Note here of course that square No. 1 is very safe and that one square may be hit a number of times whilst others escape relatively unscathed.

The rate at which the artillery fires per move is again up to the individual, but it should really bear some relationship to that of the infantry small arms – five or six times a minute is a not unreasonable rate of fire. The effect of a shellburst varies depending on whether it is a ground (i.e. impact), air or delayed firing. The wargamer can either adopt a standard burst circle indicator of say 3in. diameter or circles of varying size to reflect the different types of shell and their varying effectiveness.

Suvla Bay-fire zones

The ridge held by Turkish troops

1 2 3 4

5 6 7 8

9 10 11 12

13 14 15 16

Shore line

Suvla Bay-shell squares

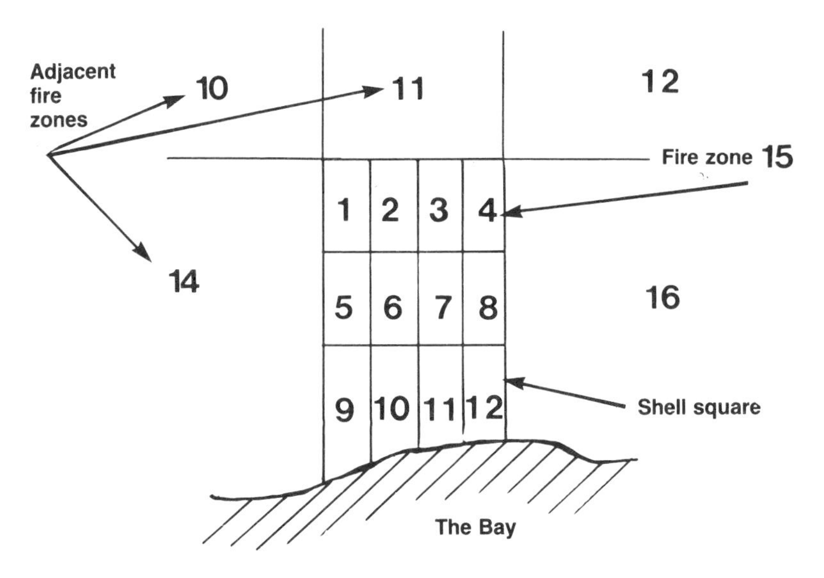

Figure 12

These shellburst indicators are easily made from thin card, acetate or even paper or wire – the number of indicators required will depend on the manner in which artillery fire is to be represented – individual common fire, full battery fire etc.

Any soldier caught in the burst circle needs a 5 or 6 on one ordinary dice to save him, otherwise he is removed from the playing area. Again, the Turks could have the benefit of only a 6 being sufficient to kill one of their number, but this may be seen as taking things too far.

So, the Allies have to fight their way across a beach and fire zone, making slow if any progress against a literally invisible enemy.

Is there any point to such a game, even if it is a solo affair? There are in fact several. It is always interesting to recreate an actual engagement and fight it through – usually such an exercise is far more enlightening than simply reading books on the subject. Further, the wargame enables the player to experience some of the problems and indeed frustrations of the soldiers and generals of the day. If required, a full-blown landing can be staged and logistics problems introduced. Stores of all kinds – ammunition, food, etc. – were landed in a fairly haphazard fashion at Suvla Bay, a situation which offers the wargamer no end of interesting avenues to follow, if required. The problems of re-supplying the troops in these conditions can cause some very real headaches.

As the Allied troops struggle across the beach-head, the fact that the Turks are not actually present becomes totally irrelevant as an unremitting barrage of fire crashes down from the heights above the bay.

Finally, there is always the chance that the Allies will gain the ridge line. If this happens, the Turks will at once quit, for the invaders will have achieved their initial objective.

As before, each rule and each situation can produce numerous others – to what degree they are pursued is entirely at the whim of the wargamer.

5 SOLITAIRE SCENARIOS

The purpose of this chapter is to offer instant battle situations and problems for the solo-player to follow through and solve. The intention is not for once to offer rule mechanisms, but for the wargamer to use his own favourite rules for the conduct of the game. Where relevant, however, a few suggested general rules are included in the scenarios. In fact it will be found to be beneficial if the rules used are both straightforward and familiar to the player, in order that the focus is on the point of the scenario rather than on game mechanisms.

The following scenarios offer a selection of problems and can be set in varying periods.

Suggested forces are listed in a couple of popular periods – Horse and Musket and Medieval. However, there is nothing to prevent the wargamer transposing the scenarios into other periods, English Civil War, late 19th century or WW2 for example, with suitable amendments to the force lists.

The unit sizes will vary according to the wargamer's own preference and thus have been omitted.

All the scenarios are designed so that they can be reasonably completed within 20 moves. If this is not achieved, then the end of the twentieth move is a convenient point at which to adjudicate the outcome.

Finally, in all the following maps, north is assumed as being at the top edge of the map.

Scenario 1 – Secure the Village Fig. 13 shows a village situated at a road junction. The surrounding hills and woods are indicated – the former cause a half speed penalty to any troops on them, the latter are impassable.

One contending force enters at point A, the other at point B. The mission of both forces is to take the village, garrison it (with one regiment of infantry) and then move on to leave the scenario at point C. In default of this being achieved and either side being unable to claim a full strategic victory, then a tactical victory can be claimed if the village is held by the end of the game.

HORSE & MUSKET	ANCIENTS
Units entering at point A	
1 light infantry battalion	1 archer or skirmishing unit
6 line infantry regiments	6 spear-armed units
3 light cavalry regiments	3 cavalry or light chariot units
1 battery of horse artillery	1 engine or elephant
Units entering at point B	
5 line infantry regiments	6 spear-armed units
1 grenadier regiment	1 armoured unit
2 medium cavalry regiments	2 half-armoured cavalry units
1 battery of horse artillery	1 engine or elephant

Scenario 2 – We want that Bridge! At the centrally placed river crossing is an inn and, to the south of this, a walled country house of some substance.

The river is fordable, but not within 18in. either side of the

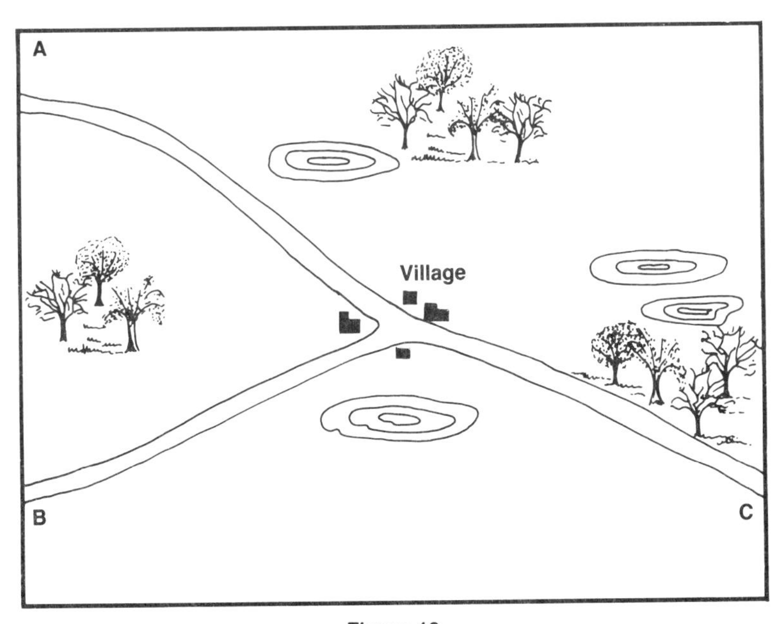

Figure 13

bridge. Troops fording, moving on hills and through the woods do so at half speed.

One force enters the map (Fig. 14) at points A and B, whilst the enemy enters at D. More enemy units arrive at point C to support the force coming on at D, but only after a delay – the score on two ordinary dice will dictate on which move these units appear. Note that point B is to the east of the river while point C is to the west.

This is an encounter battle and both forces want to control the river crossing. If either one succeeds in doing so they have won, if not they have lost. The scenario cannot really be drawn, for undisputed possession of the bridge is the whole purpose of the action.

HORSE & MUSKET	ANCIENTS
Units entering at point A	
4 line infantry regiments	4 spear-armed units
2 heavy cavalry regiments	2 armoured cavalry or heavy chariot units
2 batteries of artillery	2 engines or elephants
Units entering at point B	
1 light infantry battalion	1 archer or skirmishing unit

Two 54mm Gladiators – combats between such figures can offer extremely stimulating wargames.

2 line infantry regiments	2 spear-armed units
1 light cavalry regiment	1 horse archer, light cavalry or light chariot unit

Units entering at point C

3 line infantry regiments	3 spear-armed units
1 light cavalry regiment	1 horse archer, light cavalry or light chariot unit
1 heavy cavalry regiment	1 armoured cavalry or heavy chariot unit
1 battery of artillery	1 engine or elephant

Units entering at point D

1 light infantry battalion	1 archer or skirmishing unit
3 line infantry regiments	3 spear-armed units
1 medium cavalry regiment	1 half-armoured cavalry unit
1 battery of artillery	1 engine or elephant

Scenario 3 – Take the High Ground A ridge of hills runs east to west across the wargames table, and is situated on a line one quarter of the playing area in from the northern edge. That is to say, the

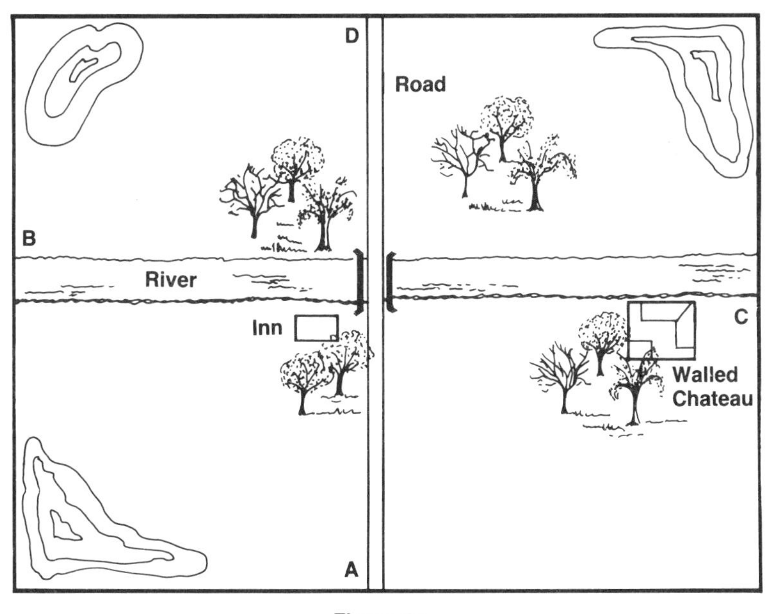

Figure 14

Colonial battles always have an element of excitement about them – these Dervishes offered stiff opposition to the British in the Sudan.

ridge would be placed one foot in from one edge of a four-feet wide playing area (Fig. 15).

The attacking force approaches the hills from the southern edge of the table. They outnumber the defenders by two to one, but have a fair amount of playing area to cover before they can come to grips.

For the purposes of the scenario the defenders must hold the line of the hills for the duration of the game and cannot expect to receive reinforcements.

The ridge line cannot be outflanked and any defenders positioned behind the crest cannot be fired at, but neither can they themselves fire.

HORSE & MUSKET	ANCIENTS
Defenders	
1 light infantry battalion	1 archer unit
3 line infantry regiments	3 spear-armed units
1 battery of artillery	1 engine
Attackers	
2 light infantry battalions	2 skirmishing units

5 line infantry regiments
1 grenadier regiment
2 batteries of artillery

5 spear-armed units
1 armoured unit
2 engines or elephants

Scenario 4 – Empire Building Territorial gains are always important to an invading army. Such gains offer potential supplies of food, cheap – if unwilling – labour and various forms of raw material. Further, it is always better to fight on someone else's country rather than your own.

Inroads made into enemy territory offer both advance bases for further assaults and buffer zones against counter-attacks.

In the following scenarios, Fig. 16 represents a deceptively peaceful scene with two small villages and one rather larger settlement. Due to the proximity of the border, each village maintains its own militia unit and there are regular troops stationed at the largest of the three communities.

More regular troops are stationed outside the playing area to the west and will march to the sound of any military activity taking place near the border.

The neighbouring state located to the east of the map has some very firm designs on securing the area for itself after casting

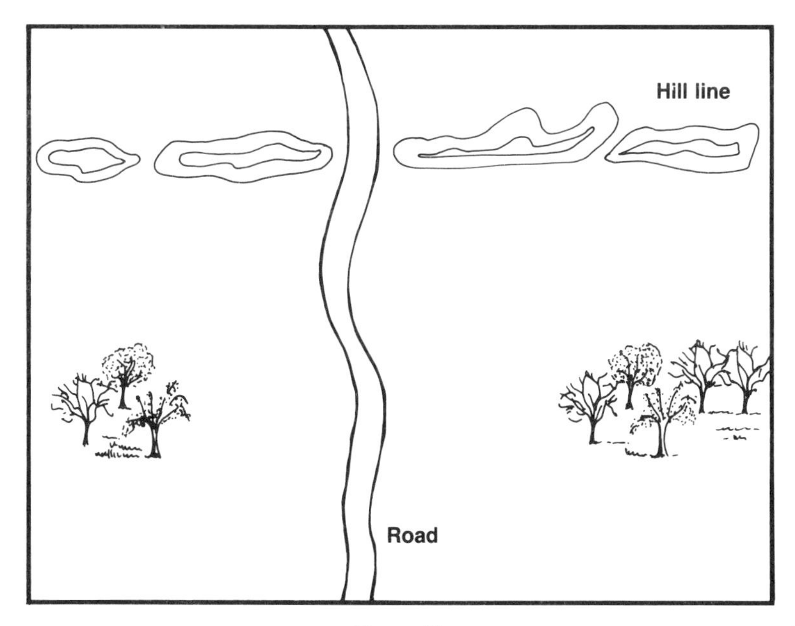

Figure 15

covetous eyes on its agricultural ability and local industries. Accordingly, a task force is raised with the intention of seizing the three villages shown on the map. Clearly the village militia cannot hope to hold out for long in the face of a determined attack, but help is not too far away. Note, however, that even with their supporting troops, the defenders are still outnumbered by the invaders. This doesn't seem unfair, because no country can maintain substantial garrisons everywhere along its borders.

HORSE & MUSKET	ANCIENTS
Defenders	
At Village A	
1 militia battalion	1 spear-armed unit with a quarter of its strength bow- or sling- armed.
At Village B	
1 militia battalion	1 spear unit with a quarter of its strength bow- or sling-armed.
At Village C	
1 militia battalion	1 spear-armed unit
1 yeomanry cavalry unit	1 light cavalry unit
1 volunteer half battery (i.e. 1 gun)	1 light engine

A medieval breech loading gun, perfect for either a siege or a field action.

Reinforcements

3 infantry regiments	3 spear-armed units
1 heavy cavalry regiment	1 armoured cavalry unit
1 light cavalry regiment	1 light cavalry unit
1 battery of artillery	2 light engines

Invaders

2 light infantry battalions	2 archer or skirmishing units
7 line infantry regiments	7 spear-armed units
1 heavy cavalry regiment	1 armoured cavalry unit
2 medium cavalry regiments	2 half-armoured cavalry units
1 light cavalry regiment	1 horse archer unit
2 batteries of artillery	2 elephants

For the purposes of this scenario, Militia and Yeomanry units are numerically two-thirds the size of their regular counterparts, and have an appropriate reduction in effectiveness. The volunteer half battery may function as a regular formation: it's quite hard to fire two thirds of a field gun!

This is a win or draw type of action. If the defenders hold any of the three villages at the end, then they can claim a draw. Should the invaders have seized all three, clearly they have won.

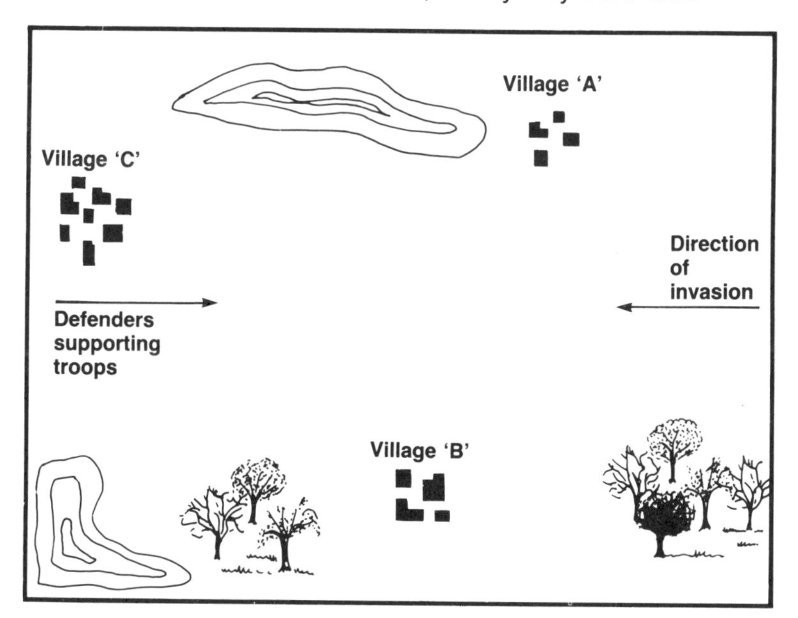

Figure 16

Something larger, a medieval bombard – an essential item of Medieval siege equipment.

Exactly on which move the defender's support troops arrive at the western edge of the playing area can be decided on the throw of two ordinary dice.

Scenario 5 – Slowly Back, and Fire! There are many battles throughout history where, if only the commanders had known the strength – or rather lack of same – of the enemy, events would have turned out somewhat differently.

In this scenario (Fig. 17), one force is heavily outnumbered and must retreat. Since however the (unrepresented) main army to the west is relying on this force as a rearguard, it may do so only slowly.

The attackers, unaware that they face only relatively few troops, also move slowly westwards as they both build up their forces and advance. Once the attackers' build-up is complete, they will overwhelm the sparse defenders. However, by the time that happens, these very defenders may well have successfully and safely made their way to the relative safety of their own (also unrepresented) main army – i.e. the western table edge.

To govern the arrival of the attackers' troops we can use the following system. Initially any two of the attacking units can be placed on the table, within one move – for their type – of its eastern edge. For the rest, three ordinary dice are used. The score on these dice indicate the move on which the particular unit in question appears at the same eastern edge.

The order of their arrival, however, can be determined by the player – let's not be too harsh!

HORSE & MUSKET	ANCIENTS
Defenders	
2 light infantry battalions	2 archer units
1 light infantry regiment	1 spear-armed unit
1 light cavalry regiment	1 horse archer unit
1 battery of artillery	1 cart-mounted light engine
Attackers	
3 light infantry battalions	3 archer or skirmishing units
6 line infantry regiments	6 spear-armed units
2 light cavalry regiments	2 horse archer units
2 medium cavalry regiments	2 half-armoured cavalry units
2 batteries of artillery	2 engines or elephants

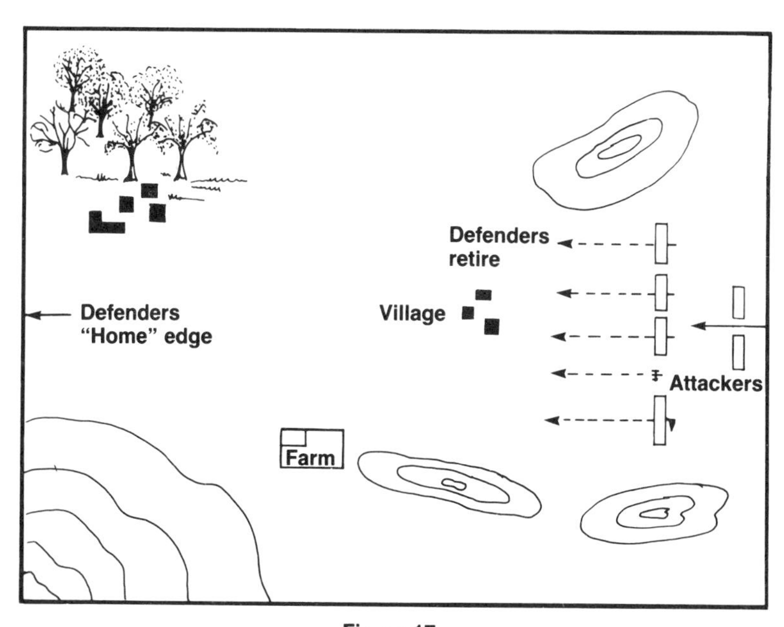

Figure 17

A protective shield from behind which the medieval gunners worked their primitive siege guns.

Scenario 6 – Messing about on the River Crossing a river by means of boat, raft or whatever can be a tricky affair, especially if such activity attracts the close attention of the enemy. Sometimes, however, it has to be done and this scenario offers a basis for just such a mission.

The main terrain feature is a fairly wide river – shall we say 9in.? – which has to be crossed. Suitable boats can either be scratchbuilt or the ubiquitous and cheap made-in-Hong-Kong plastic variety can be utilised. Each boat can in theory, if not in practice, carry a quarter of a unit, be it infantry or cavalry. Artillery or engines would not be shipped over at this stage, but would provide supportive or repressive fire from the 'home' bank. To load a quarter of a unit onto a boat takes a full move, as does the off-load. Thus neither the boat nor the men destined for it can have any movement – other than that naturally incurred by the loading process – in that move.

Once loaded, the boats can move 4½in. per move, but not straight ahead. The river current flows from right to left and will tend to push the boat to the left. Thus the rule is that for every 3in. of forward movement the loaded boat will move 1in. to the left. This does not count as part of its total move distance, and so the

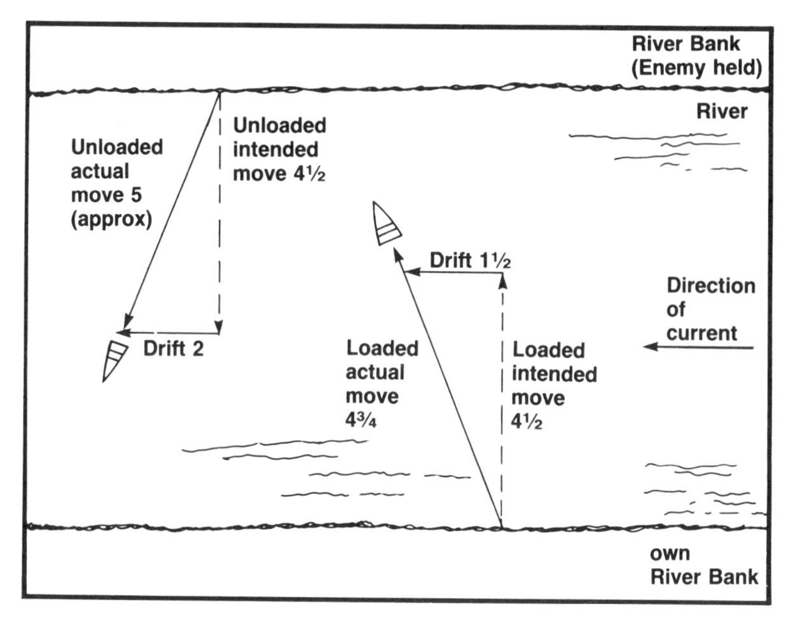

Figure 18

full move will be 4½in. out and 1½in. to the left. Fig. 18 illustrates this.

Coming back empty, the boat is even more vulnerable and for every 3in. of move will drift 2in. to the right. Any crew figures are included in the boats simply for their aesthetic value and play no part in the scenario.

The object of the action is for the attackers to land 75% of their force on the enemy bank of the river and for the defenders to prevent this. To do so, they can use firepower or forays against the landed or landing troops. There are sufficient boats only to move one and a half units at a time and the boats are vulnerable to artillery fire or stone throwing engines.

The rules in use should, with minor adaptations, cover this eventuality, but a couple of general points are worth noting. The boats should be difficult, but not impossible, to hit. Secondly the men in a boat that is hit while in mid-river can either all be lost as a result or saved individually. As a rule, swimming in full uniform in a wide and fast-flowing river is not a recommended pastime, so their chances of survival in the water should be relatively slim. If the boat is hit while loading or unloading, the men can be diced for in the normal way.

Apart from attacks from the defending forces or minor forays by the newly-landed troops, there is no physical contact between the forces in this scenario.

Once the attackers have 75% of their original force across the river, the defenders will fall back, but in any event the game is over, for the purpose of the defenders was to prevent that crossing.

HORSE & MUSKET	ANCIENTS
Attackers	
2 light infantry battalions	2 archer or skirmishing units
2 line infantry regiments	2 spear-armed units
2 light cavalry regiments	2 horse archer or spear-armed units
1 battery of artillery (in support)	2 engines (in support)
6 boats	6 boats
Defenders	
1 light infantry battalion	1 archer unit

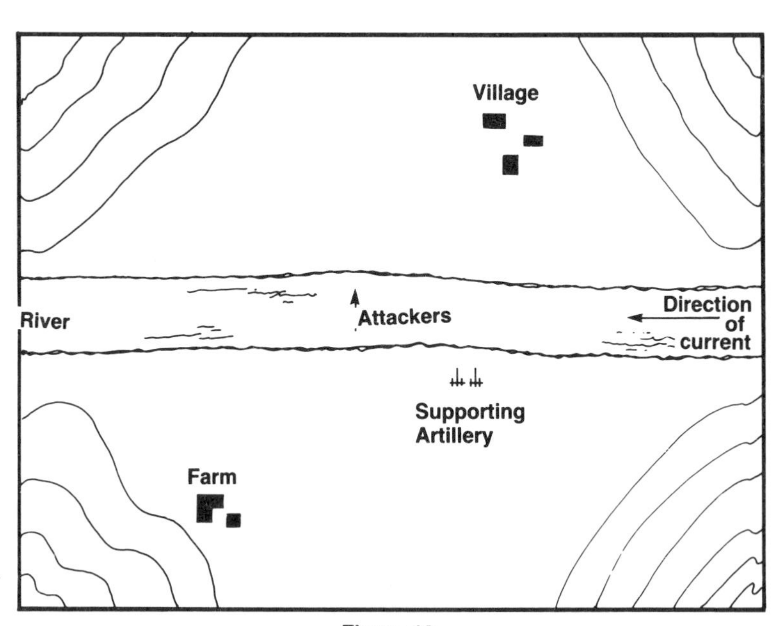

Figure 19

2 line infantry regiments	2 spear-armed units
1 medium cavalry regiment	1 half-armoured unit
2 batteries of artillery	4 engines

Scenario 7 – House Clearance a Speciality Fighting in built-up areas is a costly and time-consuming business, but there are occasions when commanders are left with no alternative course of action.

In this scenario (Fig. 20) a relatively small force of troops attempts to delay as much as possible the progress of a larger body of the enemy. To aid them in this is the fact that the defenders know the village well and have had time to prepare some defences.

The defenders cannot defeat their aggressors, but they can delay them long enough to win the scenario. If the attackers do not reach the western edge of the playing area by the end of the twentieth move then the defenders can justifiably claim a victory.

Numbers for this particular scenario should be limited. If the units specified below are found to be too parsimonious then they can be increased, but the two to one ratio should be retained.

While troop units are listed, this is one scenario which would perhaps benefit from the use of single figures, particularly for the defenders.

A farm put together using card buildings from Games Workshop and wall sections from Hovels Ltd. Such a set up can form a basis for many solo actions in a variety of periods.

HORSE & MUSKET	ANCIENTS
Defenders	
2 light infantry battalions	2 archer units
1 line infantry regiment	1 spear-armed unit
1 battery of artillery	2 engines
Attackers	
1 light infantry battalion	1 skirmishing unit
4 line infantry regiments	4 spear-armed units
1 grenadier regiment	1 armoured unit
1 medium cavalry regiment	1 half-armoured unit
2 batteries of artillery	4 engines or elephants

Scenario 8 – Wheel meet again A lightly guarded convoy of wagons has run into a spot of bother. One of the wagons has suffered a broken wheel and has had to be left behind with a guard by the rest of the convoy. On reaching their destination, the escort pass on the news about the disabled wagon. At once a relief column is organised, complete with a spare wheel to put the wagon back into service, and sets off.

Meanwhile the enemy is also interested in the immobile wagon

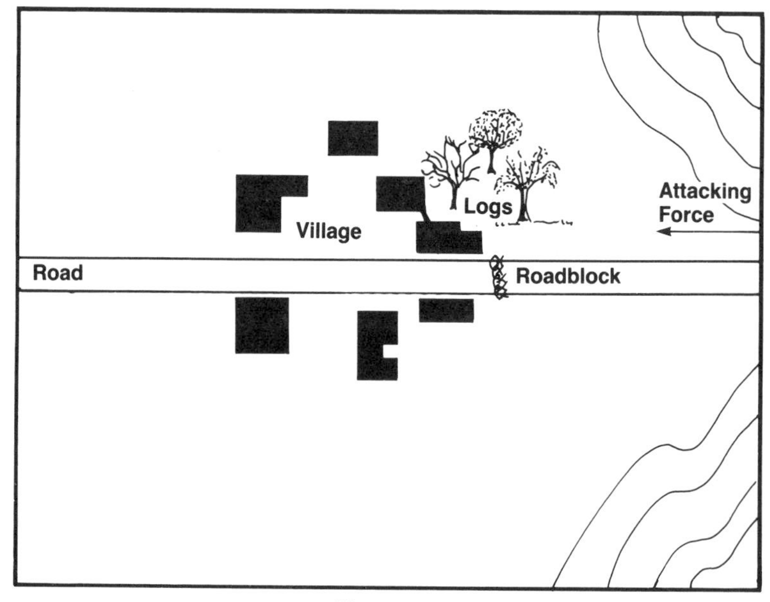

Figure 20

and its small escort and decide to investigate. The wagon guard, on the alert for just such an event, open fire on the inquisitive enemy, hoping that relief is at hand.

This scenario is fought in three stages. Firstly the wagon guards attempt to keep their attackers at bay. Next, reinforcements arrive and deploy to allow the wagon to be repaired. Finally the wagon and its new escort have to gain the safety of the eastern edge of the table once more. A moderately complex, three-part engagement follows and offers numerous permutations for the solo player.

To consider each phase: the wagon guards take up defensive positions and open fire on their assailants. Now, there cannot be too many of them; it is suggested that six figures would fit the bill adequately enough.

It seems unlikely that the enemy presence would be anything more than a scouting party and should thus consist of light troops, probably without artillery support.

Finally the relief column would be principally calvalry, although doubtless another wagon and team would be needed to carry the required wagon wheel.

The timing of each phase can be decided by the usual dice throw – perhaps one ordinary dice for the arrival of the enemy, but two ordinary dice to determine when the support column arrives.

A fairly timeless house, an invaluable item of wargames scenery and useful for many solo games.

Some minor rules for individual figures firing may well be needed but these are easily constructed: one figure firing (musketeer of archer) has a range of say 18in., the effectiveness of his shooting being split into three range bands:

0–6in.	4, 5, 6 on one dice kills
6in–12in.	5, 6 on one dice kills
12in–18in.	6 only on one dice kills

This rule can be equally applied to the defenders or the attackers. To fix the new wagon wheel in place will take two moves so the men detailed for this job will need protection by their comrades for this length of time. It is suggested that four men would be needed for the task, but they need not be specialist wheelwrights or blacksmiths etc.

	HORSE & MUSKET	ANCIENTS
Defenders	6 infantry men	6 archers
A. wagon		
B. relief column	1 light infantry battalion	1 skirmishing unit
	1 line infantry battalion	1 spear-armed unit

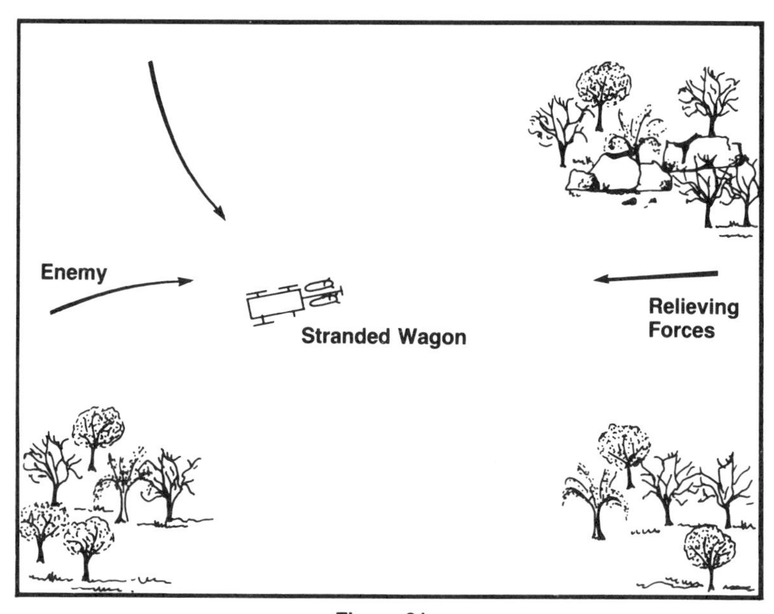

Figure 21

1 light cavalry regiment	1 horse archer unit
1 medium cavalry regiment	1 half-armoured unit
1 wagon	1 wagon

Attackers

1 light infantry battalion	1 skirmishing unit
2 light cavalry regiments	1 horse archer unit
	1 spear-armed unit

6 PROGRAMMED SCENARIOS

One of the most exciting innovations for solo wargamers in recent years has been the idea of the programmed scenario. The credit for this extremely stimulating concept belongs to my very good friend Charles S. Grant. In his book *Programmed Wargames Scenarios* (Wargames Research Group, 1983) Charles allows for both armies in a wargame to be played, both to be programmed or one to be played and one programmed. Suitable for virtually any period, the book offers the solo wargamer a fund of scenarios in which a realistic and responsive enemy can be brought to battle.

To offer a brief synopsis of the principles of Charles' book would be difficult, so I am extremely indebted to both Charles and his publishers for their permission to reproduce the bare essentials of just one small scenario here.

Hill Line Defence

INTRODUCTION This scenario presents the player with a defensive force occupying a low hill line and an attacker already deployed off the line of march and about to commence the battle.

GROUND The options for the ground are given on Figure 23 (attacker) and Figure 22 (defender) but they should not be consulted at this stage, although the terrain is diced for and recorded. In broad outline they provide a low hill line to the north of the table, some isolated features such as small villages or woods, and some approach roads to the south.

PERIOD This scenario is suitable for any period.

GENERAL SITUATION Blue force has been tasked to hold the low hill line along the north side of the table while Red force must take the feature, defeating Blue in the process, within the day. Apart from a general indication of Blue's position along the crest,

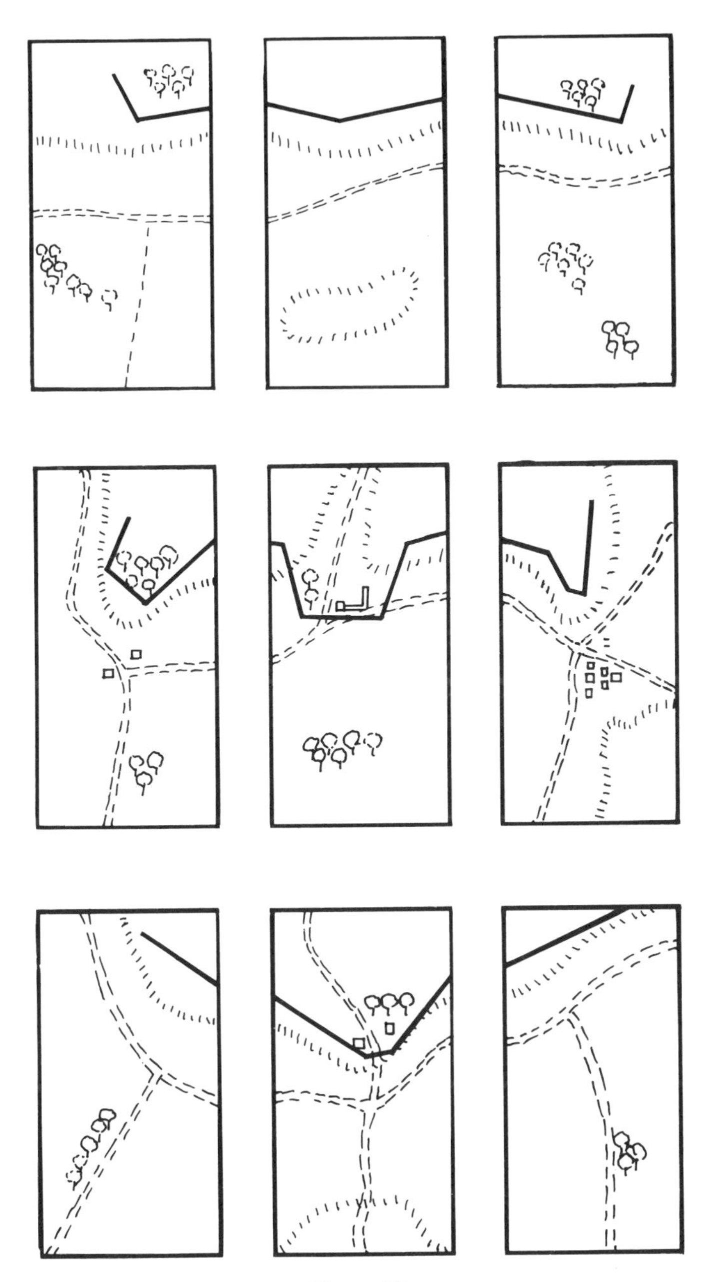

Figure 22

Red has little idea of the strength or disposition of Blue. Similarly Blue will not be aware of the nature of Red's assault.

PLAYING OPTIONS If the player intends to personally command one of the two sides he should turn to the instructions for that force next. If both sides are going to follow the programmed instructions then the player should start by reading Red Force instructions.

Blue Forces

FORCES See note at the end of this extract.

MISSION To hold the low hill line feature.

Execution

1. PLAYER'S OPTION If the Blue Force is the player's chosen force then he may deploy his forces as he sees fit up to, but not south of, the line shown on the map in Figure 22. He then writes his orders for the defence of his position. If the player is playing the Blue Force he need read no further but should turn to the Red Force instructions after completing the above requirements.

2. PROGRAMMED BLUE OPTION If the Blue Force is the programmed enemy then the player should have read the Red Force instructions, chosen his forces and may have deployed them and written their orders prior to considering the enemy in this section.

It is at this stage that the enemy commanders may be given personalities along the lines suggested in the chapter 'The Enemy'. Now we come to the deployment of the Blue Force in its defensive posture. This deployment must follow the following rules and uses the map in Figure 22.

a. No deployment south of the line given on the map in Figure 22.
b. Throw a single dice.
   1, 2 or 3 – all light troops divided equally across the front.
   4, 5 or 6 – all light troops divided equally between the flanks.
c. Throw a single dice for the deployment of the remaining forces.

(1) 1–30 per cent in centre section, 35 per cent to each flank.
(2) 2–40 per cent in centre section, 30 per cent on each flank.
(3) 3/4 – 50 per cent in centre section, 25 per cent on each flank.
(4) 5–60 per cent in centre section, 20 per cent on each flank.
(5) 6–50 per cent in centre section, 15 per cent on one flank, 35 per cent on the other

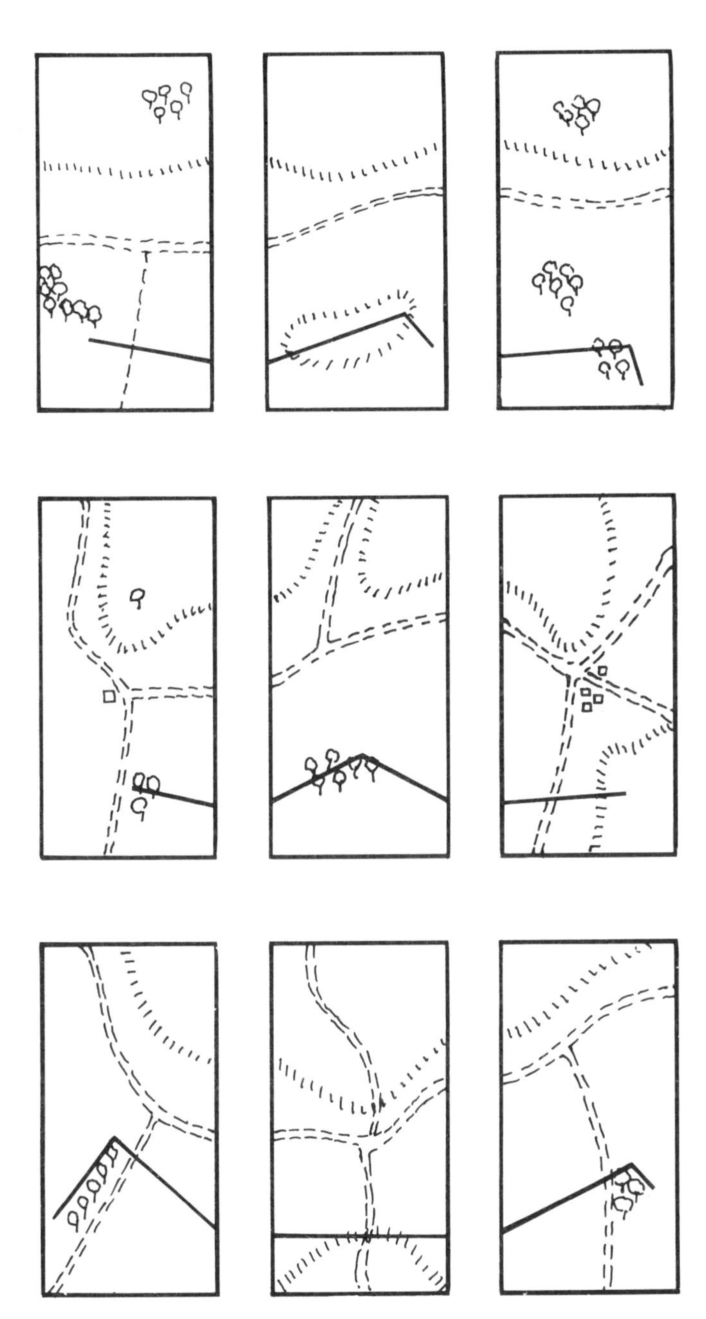

Figure 23

(to be determined by dice throw)

d. 15 per cent of the whole force, deployed in the central section of the table, must be nominated as a reserve and not deployed in the front rank.

3. PROGRAMMED BLUE ORDERS This section must not be read until Red Force has written his orders.

A single dice is thrown to determine how Blue will make his overall plan.

a. Throw 1 – Blue will hold the entire feature well forward and will give no ground, and he will not move off the contour, even to follow up, under any circumstances.
b. Throw 2 – Blue will hold the entire feature, well forward and will give no ground. However, he will follow up, even off the contour if it is to his advantage.
c. Throw 3 – Blue will give ground to maintain his lines but will not commit his reserve under any circumstances.
d. Throw 4 – Blue will give ground to maintain his line but will commit his reserve to keep the line intact.
e. Throw 5 – Blue will take the offensive wherever the opportunity offers.
f. Throw 6 – Blue will be content to retain only a part of the feature at the end of the day provided his forces are united at that location.

4. PROGRAMMED BLUE RESPONSES There are some specific responses which can be included in this game. In each case only the circumstances need be noted in advance and the responses can be read and diced for once the circumstances become fact. Once again these are decided by a dice throw and relate to three different events.

a. 'An enemy flank attack in strength reaches the edge of the ridge'
   (1) Throw 1/2 – Denude the other flank to contain the attack.
   (2) Throw 3/4 – Commit the reserve unless this is specifically prohibited by the orders.
   (3) Throw 5/6 – Weaken centre to strengthen threatened flank.
b. 'An enemy frontal attack in strength reaches the edge of the ridge'.
   (1) Throw 1/2 – Concentrate all forces in centre, giving ground on flanks unless orders specify otherwise.

(2) Throw 3/4 – Give in centre in the hope of engaging enemy from both flanks.
(3) Throw 5/6 – Commit reserve in the centre, unless specifically ordered otherwise, and maintain front.

c. 'An enemy assault made along the whole front, or simultaneously on both flanks, reaches the slopes'.
(1) Throw 1/2 – Give ground and retain line.
(2) Throw 3/4 – Concentrate on likely breakthrough points withdrawing all forces from areas not threatened.
(3) Throw 5/6 – Launch all the reserve plus whatever is available, on one section of the enemy attack.

Red Force

FORCES See note at the end of this extract.

MISSION To capture the hill line position to the north.

Execution

1. PLAYER OPTION If the player has chosen to fight as the Red Force then he will know prior to reconnaissance that the enemy, Blue, is deployed in inferior strength in a defensive position to the north along a hill line. He then chooses his forces.

He may then dice to see if he is deployed before or after detailed reconnaissance (odd being yes, even being no). If he is deployed prior to reconnaissance then he does not see the enemy but knowing only that they will be on the hill line he must deploy his forces as he sees fit but south of the deployment line given in Figure 23. If the deployment is post-reconnaissance then the player will refer to the Blue *Enemy Option* section only and deploy the enemy. He will then return to this section, deploy his forces as he desires, and then write his orders. If the reader is playing the Red Force he need read no further but should turn to the Blue Force instructions and follow them through.

2. PROGRAMMED RED OPTION If Red Force is the only programmed side then the player should have read and carried out the Blue Force instructions down to and including the *Player's Option* section before reading further. If both sides are programmed then read on. Firstly one of the recommended forces is selected either by the player or at random. Personalities are allocated to Red commanders at this point if required. The force is now deployed onto the table following the rules and using Figure 23.

a. No deployment north of the line given in Figure 23.
b. Throw a single dice –
   1, 2 or 3 – All light troops divided equally across the front.
   4, 5 or 6 – All light troops divided equally between the flanks.
c. Throw a single dice for the attack directions as given below. The number given after the direction gives the ratio of troops to table sections not including the light troops already allocated.

	Left	Centre	Right
Throw 1 Attack left	6:	3:	1:
Throw 2 Attack left and front	4:	4:	2:
Throw 3 Attack front	2:	6:	2:
Throw 4 Attack left and right	4:	2:	4:
Throw 5 Attack right and front	2:	4:	4:
Throw 6 Attack right	1:	3:	6:

3. PROGRAMMED RED ORDERS The Red Force orders are very much dictated by the force distribution and attack direction already calculated. It remains only to translate the attack direction into formal written orders. Apart from the main attack force which in each case is weighted in one or two of the three sections of the table there still remains the small force in the other sector of the table and perhaps the light troops. A dice throw will determine their activity.

a. Throw 1 or 2 – Light troops and those not in the main attack will advance to cause maximum nuisance and stretch the enemy line.
b. Throw 3 or 4 – Light troops and those not in the main attack will do little more than hold their initial line and will be cautious and unimaginative.
c. Throw 5 or 6 – Light troops and those not in the main attack will be drawn in the direction.

4. PROGRAMMED RED RESPONSES Apart from any other random response system selected from the character and chance section there are two major areas for Red response to Blue activity. In the event of one of those circumstances occurring Red dices for his response as follows:–

a. A Blue Force unit is broken or falls back creating a gap in the line.
   (1) Throw 1/2 – Push all available troops whether cavalry or infantry into the gap regardless of what is occurring elsewhere.

(2) Throw 3 – Push any available cavalry into the gap, infantry will follow their current orders or wait for fresh ones if these have been overtaken by events.
(3) Throw 4 – Push any available infantry into gap.
(4) Throw 5/6 – Hesitate two moves and then push into the gap if it remains.

b, A Blue Force of more than one unit counter-attacks off the hill feature.
(1) Throw 1 – All infantry units in small arms, missile or musketry range will recoil out of range.
(2) Throw 2/3 – Push any available cavalry only into the gap; infantry will follow their current orders or await fresh ones if these have been overtaken by events.
(3) Throw 4 – No abnormal action.
(4) Throw 5 – Any cavalry within range will attempt to charge.
(5) Throw 6 – All forces within missile, musketry or small arms range will rush forward in an attempt to come to grips.

WINNING THE GAME The victor is he who achieves his mission within the day. A failure to do so by both sides will dictate a draw.

The Forces Involved

Charles offers an extensive list of forces from which the wargamer may select an army with which to fight out this scenario. Space precludes a full listing here, but two sample armies from the Horse and Musket period are included as examples.

Blue Army:	3 units of infantry 2 units of light infantry 1 unit of medium cavalry 1 unit of light cavalry 1 battery of artillery
Red Army:	6 units of infantry 1 unit of light infantry 1 unit of medium cavalry 3 batteries of artillery 1 unit of engineers

7 SOLO CAMPAIGNS

So far we have looked at smaller actions, larger – basically defensive – battles and problematical situations for the soloist to play out and examine. While these vary radically in both approach and activity level, they are all essentially single 'one off' actions. As such they are fought in isolation and have no relationship with any preceding or subsequent battles. This is fine, of course, for such games will provide stimulating play for a day or an evening, offering much in the way of interest to the solo player. There comes a time, however, when something perhaps a little 'meatier' is required, along with a degree of continuity. Problems or mistakes in one battle need to have knock-on effect on the next, and may directly affect the outcome of subsequent actions. Indeed, an intended battle may well be refused due to the result of the previous conflict – severe casualties, shortage of ammunition etc.– whereas in the case of individual actions, battle is seldom, if ever, turned down.

A wargame campaign could be viewed as being a method of linking actions and giving them a purpose, but this is rather a case of the tail wagging the dog. Rather, the wargame campaign provides a framework for battles and various other situations to occur in a logical, related sequence.

The conduct of a solo wargames campaign can be totally absorbing and an enthralling pastime. A great deal depends on the amount of detail that the soloist wishes to cover and each player can set his own level of involvement. For example, one person might be happy to simply allot a country, say, two regiments of heavy tanks as being its wartime capability, while another person would need to calculate that country's industrial potential and size its armoured capability accordingly. Yet again, instead of the industrialisation of the country being taken for granted, that particular nation could actually be developed by the player from an initial, basically agricultural, economy. Much depends on what the individual wishes a campaign to achieve for him personally.

There is no right or wrong on this aspect of the hobby, each player tailors his activities to suit his own personal needs, facilities and, for want of a better word, pressures.

The purpose of this chapter is to outline some of the main components of a solo wargames campaign, how to go about organising the various aspects and how to use such items within the context of a campaign.

Maps and Map Making Perhaps the single most important item for the conduct of a campaign is a map. This not only records all movement – be it tactical or strategic – but also offers an instant picture of the terrain over which the campaign will be fought and a ready summary of the campaign's progress, both actual and intended.

The first job is to obtain your map and there are several ways of doing this. Firstly there are the Ordnance Survey 1:50000 scale *Landranger* series of maps. These are highly detailed, naturally, but they do have a couple of drawbacks for the wargamer. Firstly they are extremely up to date – a very desirable state of affairs for normal people, of course, but something of a disavantage for wargamers wishing to cover any period earlier than the advent of railway lines, motorways and electricity pylons! A further possible drawback is that they only cover the United Kingdom, so wargamers wanting to campaign elsewhere are not helped at all. On the plus side, the detail offered by Ordnance Survey maps is extremely comprehensive – every farmhouse is shown in rural areas, as well as hill contours, gradients etc.

Staying with official maps for the moment, the Bartholomew range of world maps will be useful to wargamers. Constructed on a scale of 1:2,500,000 the coverage of the series is very good and most of the countries required by a wargamer are to be found in the series.

Also produced by the same company is a *World Travel Series* on a scale of 1:3,000,000 – a particularly useful map in this range is one of Western Europe.

To offer an idea of comparative scales, on a 1:1,500,000 map, the Iberian Peninsula measures approximately 25ins. square (625mm), while on the 1:3,000,000 the same area measures 10ins. square (250mm).

Also available commercially are various fantasy maps, which can be utilised both for their intended fantasy usage and for non-fantasy campaigns. Quite often these maps are very well produced in full colour, making them extremely useful.

Finally commercial board games offer maps, which if sometimes limited in scope by the nature of the game involved, are still very useful.

Much will depend on the theatre of operations required by the solo player. If a historical campaign based on the Marlburian Wars is planned, there is little point in the wargamer buying say the 'Frontiers of Alusia' adventure map in the *Dragon Quest* series, fine though it may be.

Similarly, if a generalised 18th century campaign is planned then just such a map will prove to be ideal and further will prevent a great deal of preconceived ideas being put into use. If the fortress of Lille is on a map, then the wargamer is virtually compelled to lay siege to it. It is unlikely however that the same stereotype compulsions will apply when the wargamer considers towns with names like Jungbar, Korsepolis or Resmaldi.

If on the other hand a board game map depicts Western Europe, for example – and a good many do – then it is useful for any period of history from the Romans onwards.

While all are in colour, the main difference between the Ordnance Survey/Bartholomew map and the fantasy/boardgame map is that the former tend to have no grids splitting up the area of the map, but if they do they are usually very large squares. The latter are usually printed with a hexagonal grid system superimposed on them.

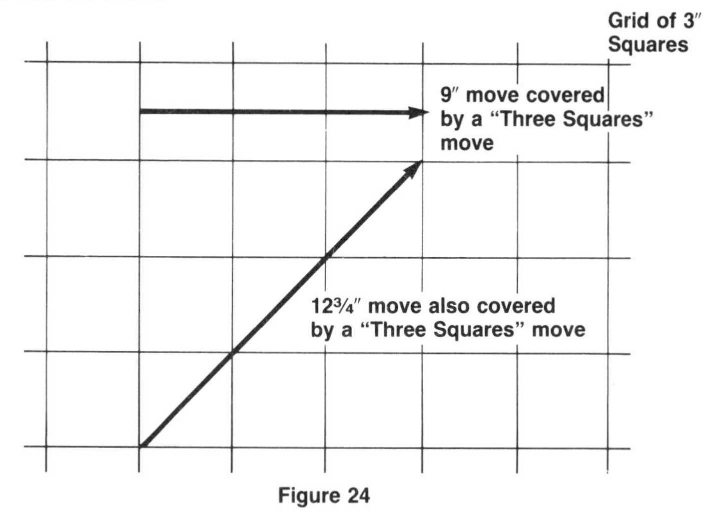

Figure 24

The square v. hexagon argument is largely one of basic geometry. The person who moves diagonally across a squared map will move faster than the player who moves horizontally, vertically or a combination of the two, as in Fig. 24.

Thus if a player can move a unit or whatever through three squares per move, by moving diagonally he can move substantially faster than someone moving horizontally.

With a hexagon grid, this problem is eradicated for all moves are rendered equal. To superimpose a hexagon grid on an Ordnance Survey map is next to impossible, unless a pre-printed overlay constructed from acetate or a similar transparent material is used.

So, the wargamer is really faced with a choice – commercial non-fantasy and a square grid, or commercial fantasy and non-fantasy and a hexagon grid.

A great deal will depend on the intended use of the map and on the theatre of war in which the proposed wargames campaign will be set. Both have much to recommend them, but each has its limitations.

Wargamers can also construct their own maps, thus totally obviating any pre-conceptions about a specific campaign. There are two starting points for this. Firstly there is the blank sheet of paper onto which can be drawn a squared grid, or there are blank sheets which are commercially overprinted with a grid of hexagons. The hexagons are available in several sizes to suit the required coverage and scale of the intended map.

Having obtained a blank sheet, square or hexagonally gridded, the next step is to design the area of operations. Once again the extent of the map's coverage will largely depend on the planned scope of the campaign. An English Civil War campaign can be fought out well enough within the confines of a county, while a WW2 action would need a considerably larger area of operations.

The map can be designed in one of three ways, as a copy of an original, as a fanciful creation or as a purely random affair.

To look at the first possibility, the map can be a copy of an existing one, suitably amended to either fit neatly onto a hexagon or square grid or to conform to the wargamer's planned strategy. This method saves a great deal of head-scratching and offers an immediate source of inspiration to the less artistic and geographically articulate wargamer. The country is already mapped, all the soloist has to do is transfer that map onto blank, gridded paper. By this means the basics of an Ordnance Survey map can be utilised, but items such as level crossings and power stations omitted. The finished map may well bear little resemblance to the original, but the basic idea and layout will have been readily provided by the first map.

For those wargamers with artistic skills, maps can be created from scratch. A coastline – if required – can be sketched in, as can perhaps a range of hills. Rivers flow from hills to sea, so their courses can be marked in. As settlements tend to spring up at suitable river crossings these can also be indicated and thus the process continues until the map is sufficiently complete to satisfy the wargamer's needs.

Finally for the wargamer who likes to create and not to copy, but lacks an artistic bent, there is the random method of establishing terrain. Under this system all the possible types of terrain are listed and are allotted a dice score. The type of dice used will largely depend on the total of the different terrain items which have been listed. Each basic type of feature – hill, town, river or whatever – can be further sub-divided and again diced for. To take a hill as an example, this may vary from mound or hillock, through small hills, to mountain ranges with cliffs and ridges thrown in for good measure.

A certain amount of 'fudging' may be needed – it is unlikely that a mountain peak would be found springing up right in the centre of a town, for example – but the basic system does offer an instant variety in terrain. A certain number of squares/hexagons can be left blank to indicate flat or open terrain and again the amount of these can be decided by the wargamer, governed by a dice throw if necessary.

Using a Map Having produced a campaign map by whatever method is chosen, the next step is to decide how to use that map for the purposes of the campaign.

Probably the first requirement is to decide on the speed of movement. Much will depend on both the scale and the scope of the map that is being used. The area covered by each square or hexagon can vary from perhaps a few kilometres or miles to several hundred, dependent on the construction and scale of the map.

Clearly, then, we cannot realistically talk in terms of hexagons or squares covered when dealing with movement. Instead, a rate of progress for the various types of soldier involved in the campaign must be decided upon and then this can be translated into the appropriate map move.

Assume for a moment that a regiment of medium cavalry can

march 20 miles (32kms) in a day. Within the context of the campaign, a 'day' implies breaking camp at first light, maintaining a steady pace for perhaps 12 hours – inclusive of halts – and then making camp for the night. It is assumed that no fighting takes place and that the unit in question is not distracted from its marching. Many factors can affect the achieved speed; the state of the roads, the nature of the terrain and the weather can all play a part in altering the actual distance covered.

If, however, the distance covered by our units is the stated 20 miles, this needs to be recorded on the map. If a hexagon (or square) is considered to be 10 miles across, then the cavalry on the march will traverse two hexagons per campaign day. Similarly, if the hexagon is scaled to measure 40 miles, then the troopers will reach only half way across a map hexagon before they encamp once more. Providing that the various speeds of the different types of unit are established, then they can readily be transferred to scale distances on the map. One point worth bearing in mind here is that it is preferable to keep distances as simple as possible. Granted an accurate scale-down of comparative speeds is a prime requirement, but the problems involved in recording achieved distance of 15¼ miles on a map square which scales out to 25 miles across can be appreciated.

A good plan is firstly to select a suitable map square/hexagon size, i.e. 20, 50 or 100 miles across. The next step is to stipulate the marching rates of the infantry, cavalry and artillery, taking care to round the produced figures up or down as required in order to make them easier to handle.

The following rates of march are suggested as a starting point, but as ever, the wargamer can alter these figures in the light of personal research and opinion.

Type of Unit	*Miles per day*	*Km per day*
Light infantry	12	19
Infantry	8	13
Light cavalry	24	38
Medium cavalry	20	32
Heavy cavalry	16	26
Horse artillery	16	26
Foot artillery	8	13
Wagons, engines etc	8	13

Bear in mind that these are optimum distances, free of enemy interference and unaffected by unfavourable terrain. The wargamer may wish to allot longer distances to guard or elite units –

this is not a problem, but it can constitute an extra and possibly unnecessary complication.

To increase the distance covered, forced marches can be allowed, but the frequency of these must be strictly governed. Any more than two consecutive days of forced marching should be judged as having a detrimental effect on the subsequent fighting ability of the troops concerned. Further, a rule could be constructed so that a forced march of two days' duration must be followed by one day of rest and two days of marching at normal speed before another forced march is allowed.

Wargamers may wish to penalise units 'marching to the guns' or becoming immediately embroiled in a battle. After one day's forced march, their fighting effectiveness could be reduced by a quarter and after the maximum two days' forced march further reduced to a half.

Thus, while forced marches can take place – as indeed they did historically – the wargamer's enthusiasm for the rapid transit of soldiers is tempered by the limiting factors. On the plus side, any unit force marching can add 50% to the distance they cover. Thus on a two-day forced march, a light infantry unit could cover 36 miles (58 km).

Dependent on period, troops can also move by rail, lorry, air transport and by water. Here the wargamer can really carry out some detailed research as to the various speeds involved – each mode of transport forms a subject in itself.

The effects on movement caused by varying terrain can be as simplistic or complex as the wargamer requires. Units can be made to move at only half speed while moving uphill or fording a river, for example. If this is found too simple, then rules can be formulated to reduce hill movement in direct proportion to the number of contour lines crossed. This stricture can be made to apply equally to uphill or downhill progress if required.

Rivers come in many shapes and sizes – narrow, wide, fast. slow, deep, shallow and each may well have its own problems. Again the half-speed rule noted above can be arbitrarily used, or more complex mechanisms can be created to cover all aspects of river crossing. Even the presence of bridges does not in fact offer the salvation that it may initially appear to – no bridge is wide enough to permit a complete army to cross in a short time and bottle-necks are inevitable as a result.

Whatever move distances and terrain limitations are used, the progress of one's units needs to be recorded on the campaign map. There are a couple of ways in which this can be achieved.

Firstly movement can be directly noted on the surface of the map. Unless this is done in pencil and subsequently erased, the map will be unusable after – or perhaps even during – the campaign.

Alternatively overlays of clear acetate or tracing paper can be used. Location reference points are noted on the overlays – usually in the corners – to ensure that they are laid over the map in the same place each time. This system has the advantage that one overlay can be produced for each of the contending forces in the campaign, if so required.

On the tracing paper ordinary or coloured pencils or felt tip pens can be used, whereas acetate requires the use of chinagraph pencils or special pens. These are available in several colours, so there is no real problem, although such implements tend to cost more than ordinary pencils or pens.

Contacts, Battles, Sieges

If the wargamer is using a single overlay sheet over the campaign map then the progress of the contending forces in furtherance of their orders is readily visible. The great pitfall here, however, is that the solo player can be tempted to influence the movements of one side to avoid or cause a contact between the forces involved, whichever is required.

Two separate overlays eradicate this to an extent and it is not until both are laid on top of the map, one on the other, that any contacts become apparent.

Once a contact between contending forces has been established, the wargamer is then presented with a situation to resolve. Firstly, perhaps, it may be important to stipulate just what comprises a contact.

The simplest way is to state that opposing forces entering the same map square or hexagon are in contact and may react accordingly. Of course, map hexagons may be some 40 scale miles across and the wargamer may wish to reduce this distance before allowing a contact to take place. A minimum distance at which opposing forces still do not see one another is difficult to quantify. A good deal will depend on the terrain – two armies could only be a mile apart, but if between them is a mountain, then they will never see one another. In a desert on the other hand, a sand cloud caused by troop movement will be visible for many miles. It is really up to the individual to decide on maximum and minimum distance of detection and doubtless these will alter throughout the campaign as conditions change.

When a contact is established – at whatever distance is deemd suitable – one of two events can take place. One side can retreat and thus avoid a confrontation or both sides can press on and bring about a battle.

Should one side wish to withdraw – due perhaps to overwhelming odds or an unfavourable terrain – then it should be allowed to do so. Granted, some battles did take place under such conditions and should the wargamer so wish it, can do so once again within the context of the campaign. Bear in mind however that one – or indeed both – the forces in contact may only be the forward reconnaissance elements of an army and these could actually seek to avoid contact in order to fulfil their proper roles and report the presence of the enemy to the main body of their respective armies.

As an aside, to fight out a skirmish action between opposing light cavalry or perhaps armoured car patrols or similar can provide an enjoyable wargame – it all depends on the involvement and detail that the wargamer wishes to draw from the campaign.

The two forces in contact may be of rather more substance than reconnaissance elements and one side really does not wish to withdraw. Such actions will at once countermand any written orders the troops were following on a strategical basis as they react to the new situation.

Should one army be caught retreating and forced into a fight, or indeed if both sides desire an action, then a battle will result. This is generally the time when the focus of attention shifts from the campaign map to the wargames table.

The principal or relevant geographical features which appear on the map are recreated as closely as possible on the table. The forces involved are then if necessary scaled down to a constant ratio and deployed either in keeping with their situation on the map by one of the random methods discussed earlier, or in accordance with the solo player's concepts.

The action can then be fought out as a table top action in the normal way, using whichever set of rules the wargamer chooses.

Sieges can occur in a campaign, although much will depend upon the period in question.

These can either be resolved very quickly by means of a dice throw, or by a more protracted method of recreating the siege itself.

Within the context of a campaign the former method is probably preferable producing as it does a quick solution. The dice throw can be based on several factors which pertain to the particular siege in question. Some suggested areas for thought are:–

1. Has the town/castle/citadel ample food?
2. Is it well garrisoned?
3. Are the troops good quality or militia?
4. Are the walls stone/brick/earth etc.?
5. How many days can the besieged last?
6. For how long can the attacker afford to maintain the siege?
7. Is there any possibility of a foray out by the defenders or a relief army arriving?
8. Does the attacker wish to stage a full siege or can the garrison simply be contained by a token force?

And so the questions go on. The answers to these will either offer a list of pluses or minuses or a list of the probable outcomes of each question. The wargamer can then decide on the result of the siege. In all perhaps half an hour's work, although the system suggested could be simplified still further if required.

To stage a full siege is both fascinating and time-consuming. The author well remembers staging the siege of Barcelona in the summer of 1987 whilst recreating the War of Spanish Succession in Spain (1702–1713). While events were largely based on the actual campaign, I cheated and moved the Duke of Marlborough himself to the area to lead the Allied armies. Historically Barcelona capitulated as soon as the neighbouring Fort Montjuich fell, but my French commanders were made of sterner stuff and the city only surrendered after a two-month siege.

It was an interesting project, but the campaign virtually came to a halt for two months as the siege was occupying the wargame table.

Clearly then, sieges are very much up to the individual campaigner and can occupy as much or as little of the action as is required; they are considered in more detail in the following chapter.

The Campaign Diary While all movement could be recorded on the campaign map, there remains a need to log the results and casualties of battle, supply details etc., and this is where the campaign diary comes into use.

There are several ways to design a campaign diary. The wargamer can purchase an exercise book and mark it out into the appropriate sections, use a loose leaf ring binder to which additional sheets can be added as required, or an old but unused desk diary can be utilised. A desk diary is suggested because a fair bit of room will be needed on each page and a pocket diary will, in all probability, be too small. A point worth making perhaps is that it does not have to be current year's diary. There is no need to pay out a lot of money for a large format diary when, in six months' time, when no one wants a diary, they can be had for a fraction of the original asking price. All that is needed is the twelve months etc. which are adaptable to wargame campaign purposes. Purists may argue as to the actual existence of February 29th in the specific campaign year in question, but one can take a point too far perhaps. . . .

In the campaign diary everything pertinent to that campaign is recorded. Movement, battles, casualties, order transmission, re-supply etc. can all be logged in the appropriate place. Let us assume for a moment that a regiment of infantry moves, within the context of some campaign manoeuvre or other, 10 miles, fights an action against local guerillas and makes camp. The distance covered, casualties suffered and supplies used by this unit all need to be logged.

Initially, at the onset of the campaign, it will be found that fairly large units – divisions, corps, legions or what you will – can be recorded. Eventually, though, the units will become smaller as brigades or garrisons are detached or even patrols sent out on various missions. Here the campaign diary becomes more complex, but providing the varying units are clearly identified within its pages, few problems will be encountered.

Also, a campaign can commence at any date, not necessarily January 1st, so a commercially produced diary will be of value in recording the day by day moves whenever the campaign begins.

It is worth repeating that everything pertaining to the campaign is recorded in its pages. All aspects – those already covered, those featured below and yet others which will occur to the individual player – should be carefully written up.

It is fascinating to mull over the story of the campaign as it unfolds in the pages of the diary. The book will act as a permanent record of events and will, if required, serve as a memory aid when it comes to awarding battle honours and promotions etc. The diary may also show where the campaign failed and will serve as a useful guide when hostilities re-open.

Supplies The two main commodities necessary to an army in the field – ammunition and food – will be considered here, but it will be readily apparent to the wargamer that there are many, many more aspects involved in re-supply. Cavalry re-mounts, blacksmiths, motor transport repair shops, medical facilities and pay, for example, can all be covered in as much or as little detail as required by the individual.

Ammunition The term ammunition is used in its very broadest terms here. Specific items in question can be arrows, crossbow bolts, javelins, hand grenades or 7.62mm bullets – the principles hopefully remain the same.

Each soldier in the field carries a limited amount of ammunition for his personal weapon. Each unit of soldiers is usually supported by some type of first line transport ammunition train, generally allocated at regimental level. Also available are reserve supplies, controlled at a higher formation level and issued to the troops either on urgent request or at the decision of a suitably high ranking officer.

The wargamer now has to quantify all this and much will depend on the period in question. To take the early nineteenth century as an example, the average infantryman of the period carried 60 rounds of personal ammunition (*Firepower*, B.F. Hughes. A & AP, 1974). This was found to be adequate for most battles, but a careful record of ammunition expenditure needs to be kept, so that the degree of replenishment required by units can be recorded. This re-supply will come from the first line transport which in turn will make good its defects from the reserve supplies.

Much will depend on the rules in use. If one wargames figure represents 25 actual soldiers, then every time that figure fires, 25 rounds/arrows or whatever are used. To carry on with our example, however, that same figure should be equipped with $25 \times 60 = 1500$ rounds to start with. When figures become casualties it is probably easier to assume that any ammunition they had on them is lost. Rules can be formulated for its retrieval of course, but are likely to be unnecessarily complex. The added refinement can be needed in the latter stages of a compaign when supply lines are extended and units are short of everything. Using re-supply rules, the loss of an ammunition wagon due to a direct hit by the enemy's artillery or perhaps a successful raid mounted for just that purpose can have dire effects on the wargamer's war plans and campaign strategy generally.

It is unlikely that one's units will need re-supply during an actual battle, so we are really considering the strategical aspects in this section.

It is probably necessary to stipulate whether or not ammunition is interchangeable. This does not really apply to a pre-gunpowder period on the grounds that an arrow is an arrow, a spear a spear.

However, do the musket balls of your forces fit the weapons of the enemy and vice versa? It is a point worth considering and making a decision on during the very early stages of the campaign.

In addition the various calibres of artillery in use need to be documented to try to prevent the incorrect ammunition being issued to a particular battery. This is true of any period – there is very little purpose in delivering a supply of large bolts to a stone-throwing engine.

The ultimate re-supply comes from one's home base. This fact raises a couple of intriguing questions for the solo campaigner. Has the base the capacity to produce the required amount of ammunition and, secondly, as supply lines extend, will the new shipments reach the field armies?

The former may be considered to be outside the context of the campaign, but can offer the wargamer an interesting problem to solve. The question of re-supply reaching the front line can be settled by the use of both base and advances supply dumps and adequate line of communication protective troops.

As with all aspects of campaigning, the depth of coverage and detail is very much up to the individual, but the ammunition question is a most important point and is worth a good deal of consideration.

Restrictions on its use and the governing of re-supply can add a very stimulating element to any campaign and indeed can have a direct influence on both its conduct and outcome.

Food 'An army marches on its stomach' Napoleon is reputed to have said. Certainly the Peninsular War (1808–1814), where large armies starved and small armies were defeated, served to underline this point.

We can have our wargames units burdened down with ammunition, but if they have not eaten in three days, they are unlikely to give their best.

The amount of food available to an army is largely dependent on two main factors: the ability of the land over which the army marches to support that army and the army's own self-sufficiency.

Clearly, if an army is operating in a desert or similarly barren environment then food will be far more of a problem than would be the case if Western Europe was the theatre of war. A fair bit of paperwork is involved in the keeping of food consumption/availability records, but this is a very important aspect of campaigning.

While we are considering food for the soldiers themselves here, it is worth bearing in mind that camels, horses, and elephants used by the military all need feeding. Indeed prior to the twentieth century the campaigning season was usually limited to the period May to September each year, due to the need for horse fodder to be available before operations could begin.

The modern successors of the horse, the tank and similar vehicles, also need their 'food' in the shape of 'POL' – petrol, oil and lubricants. Whilst falling outside the scope of food proper, the continuing supply of these essential items is also a constant problem in modern conflicts.

Returning to food, the first parameter to establish is the amount of food consumed by one soldier (and his mount?) in a 24 hour period. Once this is decided then all other necessary calculations can be made.

As a basis for thought and to obtain some idea as to the size of the problem, let us assume that the average soldier – of whatever period – consumes 2lb of meat and 1lb of bread a day. Thus 1,000lb of meat and 500lb of bread will be required to feed a unit of 500 men for the same period and a somewhat alarming 7,000lb of meat and 3,500lb of bread for a week.

Now there are three methods by which an army in the field can obtain food. There is the ability of the army to make its own food – 'meat' on the hoof can accompany the army and bread can be baked in camp each evening. Alternatively the individual units can scrounge what they can from the surrounding countryside and finally there is always the possibility of re-supply from base, but this is far less likely in the case of food. Usually armies were expected to fend for themselves once they had set off at the start of a campaign.

To be self-sufficient, an army would need to be accompanied by a considerable number of animals intended for slaughter – which in turn, of course, also need to be fed.

Bread can be baked in the camp, but flour or wheat will be needed before this is possible, so this also has to be carried.

Really, the record of the food available to an army forms a two-part entry in the campaign diary. On the one side the food consumed by the army is countered by the food still available. While the former is relatively constant i.e. dependent on the number of men in the field, the latter can be subject to many variables. It is all very well to have beef cattle accompanying the army, but just how many soldiers can one cow feed and for how long? Also, what if the beast has been on the march for some time and is no longer the plump and healthy animal it once was? The supplies of flour can become infected by weevils and be rendered unusable or equally can be ruined by rain. Cattle can be driven off by the enemy – and equally so 'liberated' from them! Once again, the opportunies for the wargamer to explore every facet of supplying an army in the field with food are immediately presented by virtue of a campaign. It is all very well to say an army 'lives off the land' but for just how long will an area of land – of what size? – support 'x' hundred men? A change in position could be forced on the army not through any action by the enemy but by the need to move on to seek fresh land to exploit in order to produce food for its soldiers.

Such are the pressures of a campaign.

The Weather The weather, or rather its effects, is one of the most difficult aspects to simulate in a wargame. Clearly deep snow or heavy rainfall will reduce movement, but there again so will a prolonged period of high temperature.

It is not easy to imagine one's miniature figures trudging through knee high snow when the table they are crossing is covered in green terrain and there is July sunshine streaming in through the window of the wargames room.

In the author's experience, the only effects that the weather has on a wargame are adverse. As a result muskets cannot fire, bowstrings become damp etc. – it is all very depressing stuff! At one stage I adopted a policy that whatever the real weather was doing that day, then my campaign weather was doing the same. This is fine, but since the campaign was a solo affair the periods of involvement varied and often had long intervals between them, so some curious weather resulted!

This method does have much to recommend it, however, and saves a good deal of paperwork. An alternative is, if possible, to study the weather records of the campaign area. Here sometimes one has to generalise since it is difficult to find precise information relating to just one part of a foreign country.

Anywhere in Western Europe can reasonably be compared with the United Kingdom in terms of weather, but after this, things are somewhat more awkward. One useful source of reference is the world temperature/rainfall/sunshine charts which feature in the pages of some of the national newspapers. These usually only quote the particular country's capital, but at least an indication as to the weather is offered as a result. Most atlases produce maps of the world indicating climates in various areas and travel books are a useful source of information.

Just what the wargamer does with the weather is up to the individual. As noted above, the usual effects are detrimental – movement reduced, fighting capabilities lowered etc. The purist will say that the weather does have a bearing on events military and that this should be reflected in a campaign. Fair enough and a valid point. The author, however, has found that there are enough problems inherent in conducting a wargames campaign without worrying overmuch about the weather.

As ever the wargamer will put his or her own interpretation on the situation and decide for themselves the degree of involvement required.

Casualties The final aspect of campaigning that will be covered is that of casualty replacements.

After every action there will be casualties. Usually in a wargame any soldiers laid low by firing or hand to hand combat are considered to be killed and that is an end to it.

In a campaign, however, a more sophisticated system may be required.

After a battle the casualties for both sides are noted in the campaign diary and the new strengths of each unit noted, where appropriate.

Now the soldiers laid low can, if required, be divided into four categories: dead, seriously wounded, immobilised and walking wounded.

The 'dead' figures are gone for good, but the other three types of casualty can possibly be returned to their units – eventually.

A base hospital needs to be established, along with forward casualty clearing stations. The seriously wounded and immobilised soldiers need to be conveyed to the base hospital, while the walking wounded can be dealt with by the forward casualty stations. Generally speaking, the walking wounded can rejoin their units after one week, those immobilised after a month and the serious casualties after six months.

Allowances must also be made for the time taken to convey the casualties to the hospital, as well as for the return trip. It is unlikely that a unit will still be in the same place as it was a month or six weeks ago.

All this can make for some complicated book-keeping in the campaign diary, but casualties are a factor in warfare and allowances should be made for them.

Drafts of troops to replace casualties can also be considered. Again, these will have to be made as to their estimated travelling time. A further complication is that there are never enough replacements and if there are, they are rarely, if ever, seasoned troops.

The effectiveness of a unit can be influenced both by the number of casualties it has suffered and the replacement troops received. Clear and concise book-keeping in the campaign diary will help, but the soloist will find this a most taxing and time-consuming aspect of conducting a campaign.

8 SIEGE WARFARE

By their very nature sieges lend themselves ideally to solo play – one side placed in a relatively static position, the other side somewhat more flexible. In the previous chapter we saw the basic outline of a siege, its overall placing within the context of a wargames campaign and its relevance to that campaign. In this chapter it is proposed to look at sieges in greater detail and to offer more ideas for the conducting of them in miniature. While the following suggestions are based on recreations using model soldiers, there is absolutely no reason why sieges cannot successfully be worked out either on paper or on a playing surface using card counters and symbols.

Sieges Through History

As long as there has been warfare there have been sieges, as one army attempts to dislodge the other from its stronghold. The history of siege warfare reflects that of field battles in that it follows a never ending story of weapon and counter. As the attackers invent some new assault weapon, so the defenders find a method of neutralising it. Similarly, as defences improve, new developments in siege craft are found to overcome them.

Probably the popular conception of a siege is that of a castle under attack from a variety of stone throwing engines and wheeled siege towers. In fact, as the following brief survey is designed to illustrate, every period of history has had its share of sieges.

The reader is probably familiar with the semi-legendary siege of Troy in the 12th century BC. The Greek attackers, foiled by the immense walls which surrounded the place, took the place by subterfuge using the celebrated wooden horse.

The Sumerians (3000–2500 BC) were innovators of siege warfare and probably invented a number of assault devices. These were further improved by the Assyrians (1100–612 BC), who were more skilful still, and better organised than the Sumerians.

Alexander the Great was a successful exponent of siege warfare and he conducted several sieges including those of Gaza and Tyre in 332 BC in his wars against the Persian empire. During the series of wars waged between Rome and Carthage, the Carthaginian General Hannibal laid siege to the Spanish city of Saguntum in 219 BC. This action was directly responsible for bringing about the second of the wars between the two powers.

Julius Caesar was another exponent of siege warfare and in his campaigns in Gaul during 58–51 BC, mounted a number of sieges, including those of Aduatuca, Alesia, Avaricum and Gergovia. Probably the most famous of these is Alesia, which involved the construction of extensive siege works by the Romans. The defending Gauls under their leader Vercingetorix surrendered and this defeat was instrumental in breaking the Gallic resistance to Roman rule.

Moving on in time, Attila the Hun besieged the French town of Orleans in 451 AD. Just as the defenders were on the point of capitulating, a relief column arrived and the decisive battle of Chalons ensued. The north Italian town of Ravenna was besieged for three and a half years from 490 AD by the Ostrogoths as they over-ran all of Italy. It was a naval blockade that finally induced the defenders to sue for peace as the country came under Gothic rule. The city of Constantinople was first besieged in 717 AD as the Moslem and Byzantine cultures clashed at the point where, traditionally, east meets west. The successful defence of the city was of vital importance since it saved Christian Europe from a Moslem invasion. The first decisive assault on the city, which ended the Byzantine empire, was in fact made early in the 13th century by troops of the fourth Crusade (1202–1204), supported by the Venetian navy.

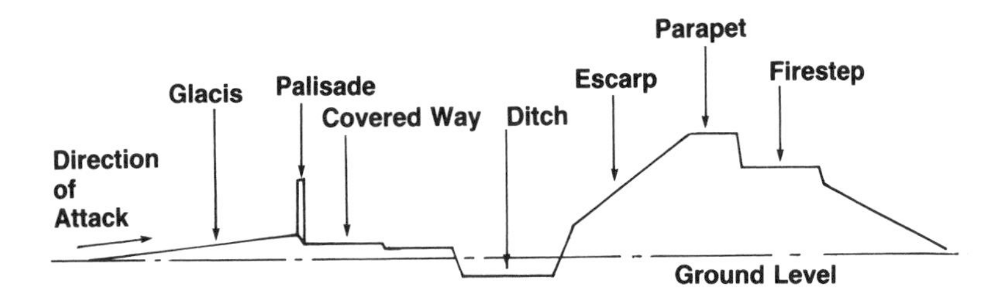

Figure 25 A cross-sectional view of a typical 18th century fortification

Late in the 9th century AD, Paris was besieged by a Viking army. This was regarded by many historians as the high point of Viking military power in Western Europe. The siege lasted for nearly a year, until the attackers were bribed to withdraw. Ten centuries later, the city was once more under siege, this time as a result of the 1870–1871 Franco-Prussian War. On this occasion, the garrison and civilian population surrendered to their German aggressors.

The Crusades, referred to briefly above, produced a number of sieges throughout their long history. The first Crusade (1096–1099 AD) for example, saw the sieges of Antioch, Jerusalem and Nicaea. The first named is particularly interesting for it was besieged twice in quick succession. On the first occasion it was the Crusaders who managed to take the city, only to find themselves immediately besieged as a Moslem relief army arrived.

As a starting point to the Agincourt campaign of 1415, Henry V laid siege to the French port of Harfleur in order to provide his army with a supply base. The town duly fell, but due to disease in addition to the fighting, the English army suffered many casualties. In 1480–81, Turkish forces besieged the eastern Mediterranean island of Rhodes, but were repulsed by the defending Knights of St. John. Some years later in 1522, the Turks, led by Suleiman the Magnificent once more laid siege to the island. After much fierce fighting, the Knights evacuated Rhodes and moved to Malta. Here however, in 1565, the Knights were once more besieged by a Turkish army. The Grand Master of the Knights, one Jean de la Valette, conducted an active defence and the arrival of a supporting Spanish fleet caused the siege to be lifted. Interestingly enough, Malta was also besieged during the Napoleonic Wars and no less surely again during the early years of World War II. For the gallantry of its people during this second conflict, the island was very fittingly awarded the George Cross.

The 18th Century was noteworthy for its sieges, as commanders on all sides sought to avoid pitched battle wherever possible in order to preserve their armies. The following century had a lesser number, but events such as the sieges of Badajos (1812), Delhi (1857) and Sebastopol (1854) were important actions.

The American continent witnessed few sieges of any consequence, but that of Yorktown in 1781 saw the end of the American War of Independence, and that of Vicksburg by Union forces in 1863 was an important part of their eventual victory. One should not overlook the Alamo, where in 1836, a handful of defenders faced a far more numerous Mexican army.

During World War II the sieges of places as far apart as Leningrad and Tobruk took place, and it should be said that during the opening years of the war Great Britain herself was under a state of siege during the Battle of Britain. After World War II, France hung on to her colonies in south east Asia. In 1953, communist-backed guerrilla forces surrounded the French held village and air strip of Dienbienphu. After a seven month siege, the defenders' positions were over-run and the French dominance over Indo-China was ended. In that same theatre of war in 1968, American forces in Khe San were under close siege from some 20,000 North Vietnamese troops for four months.

It may be seen then, that every period of history has had its fair share of sieges. Whichever period the wargamer selects therefore, will have a siege situation to offer. What is needed now is an examination of the general points on the conduct of a siege, which are common to all periods.

General Points

In order to have a siege, one must possess something which is worth the trouble of besieging and be capable of withstanding that siege. The art of fortification is a very old one – it was well advanced in the Middle East as long ago as 1000 BC. Even then, the larger cities boasted great walls which protected the inhabitants and kept out unwanted invaders. Thus any aggressors were faced with the choice of either battering down the walls, or sealing the defenders within them and waiting until they ran out of food or water. In the latter case, siege works would be built around the town or fortress which was under attack. The first recorded instance of this was the siege of Plataea in 429–427 BC. Here the Spartan and Theban attackers constructed lines of contravellation which both surrounded the city and provided the besiegers with cover. To protect the attackers themselves from being assaulted, lines of circumvallation were also built. These faced outwards and provided a defence against any relieving army which might appear. Thus the besiegers could carry out their plans, safely based between two lines of defences, one inward looking, the other facing outwards.

So, assuming for the moment at least that the attackers intend to batter their way in rather than wait for the defenders to run out of supplies, we need to look at both the defences and some ways of reducing them.

Mons Meg, Edinburgh Castle.

Defence Works

The simplest of all defence works perhaps, is the wall. This can be made from a variety of materials, dependent on where the fortification is situated. Most medieval castles had double walls, each constructed from large pieces of stone, with the cavity between them filled with tightly packed rubble. This method of construction, plus the sheer height of the walls, made them an imposing obstacle. Walls however, were not only of stone. The numerous hill forts which are to be found throughout the British Isles are made purely of earth. Some of them date from before 2000 BC and can be quite complex in design. While some examples boast only a single earth wall, others have line after line of them, offering a quite sophisticated form of defence. Usually the forts were sited on natural defensive positions such as hills or the ends of ridges. This offered a good starting point to assist the security of the earthwork. It is important not to underestimate the value of packed earth which will, hastily moving on a few centuries, absorb the impact of cannon balls and is impervious to fire. We find earthworks all through history, notably in the Dark Ages, the English Civil Wars and the 18th/19th centuries. The mighty Tower of London began life as a rudimentary earthwork sited beside the River Thames by the Normans in 1066, and the Maginot Line, constructed along France's eastern border in the late 1930s, can be seen, in its simplest form, as a reinforced earthwork.

Similar to the earth wall is one made from turf. Hadrian's Wall was originally constructed using this material and the Antonine Wall further north was only ever made from turf. Both the earth wall and the turf wall could be topped with a palisade of wood as an extra defensive measure. Further, as the wall is thrown up a ditch is created at the same time, thus contributing to the overall effect. The gates to earthworks along with any internal buildings would also be of wood. Sun-hardened mud was frequently employed in those countries whose climate permitted its use – India, Mexico, North Africa and Spain spring to mind as examples.

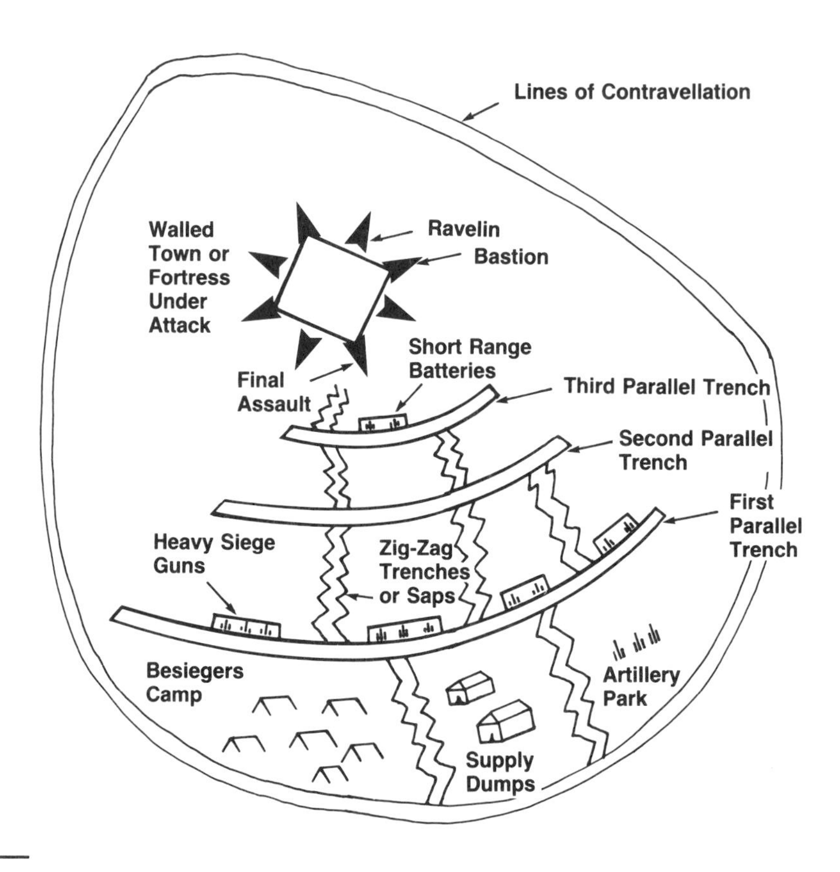

Figure 26 A typical 18th century Siege

The early castles, forts really, in the British Isles were of timber. A wooden tower, possibly sited on a hillock would be surrounded by a wooden palisade, set with a gate. William the Conqueror brought pre-fabricated wooden forts of this type with him in 1066 when he invaded England. Wooden forts are often to be found in the frontier regions of America in such actions as the American War of Independence (1775–1783) and the US Indian Wars (1850–1898).

Various other materials can also be utilised to form defensive walls – brick, concrete and sand bags and barbed wire, all means of constructing defences.

A continuous defensive wall was not however a practical proposition on a day to day basis. Access to the town or castle was needed and thus breaks in the wall had to be created to permit this. Potentially, such gaps in the wall constitute a weak point. As noted above, the gates in an earth fort were of wood and doubtless substantial baulks of timber were employed in their construction. Strong as they were, such gates could be set on fire or forced open, and so the entrances to a defensive work were fortified and became known as gatehouses, often miniature castles in themselves.

To further increase the strength of the walls, towers were built into their length at intervals, and the presence of these offered two advantages to their defenders. Firstly, since they usually projected outwards from the surface of the wall, towers enabled the garrison to inflict a flanking fire on anyone assaulting the wall itself. Secondly, they reduced the lengths of plain wall sections, thereby adding to the strength of the defences. Towers were also placed at wall corners and thus formed a conveniently strong angle.

Within the confines of the perimeter wall was the object of all this protection, either a town or the dwelling of a nobleman. In the case of the town, there would probably be a central citadel or strong point which had several uses, forming a safe refuge or second line of defence and an extra degree of firepower, since its walls were usually higher than those of the perimeter.

Similarly in a castle, the principal building within the walls would be the keep. This would house the chief occupants and its walls would tower over those on the outer edges of the defences. Here again, as with the gatehouse, the keep or citadel would be constructed as a self-contained fortress. Even if the outer walls fell, there was the keep to be overcome before the castle fell.

Many forts and castles, including earthworks, provided the

defenders with several lines of walls, each successively higher than the last, as the lines neared the centre of the complex. Thus as one wall was breached, the defenders fell back to the next and poured fire on their attackers. Since fortifications are generally designed to face outwards, anyone trapped within their confines and being fired on from inside is in for a hard time indeed. Quite often, gateways and outer lines of defences were made deliberately complicated to confuse attackers and to offer the defenders the maximum time and opportunity to fire at them.

Frequently the entire castle would be surrounded by a wide, deep ditch, which could either be dry or filled with water to provide yet another deterrent to would-be assailants. In later times, such as in World War II and Vietnam, such a ditch would be replaced by minefields.

Finally, if the defensive position was not already sited in a clear area, the ground near it would be cleared so that it did not afford cover to an attacker. A good example of this is the American fire-base or camp in Vietnam, where the jungle would be completely cleared away up to several hundred yards from the camp itself.

All this may sound pretty formidable, so now we will look at the various methods available to overcome these awesome defences.

The Engines of War

There are three ways of assaulting a defensive work, over, through or under.

In order to cross over a wall, large wooden towers on wheels were often built 'on site' so to speak. These could be moved – albeit slowly – up to the castle walls and a ramp lowered to permit the soldiers inside to dash out onto the walls and attack the defenders.

One engine which was capable of hurling stones over a wall and into the defences beyond was the mangonel, or trebuchet as it was sometimes called. Powered by a counter-weight, this was the predecessor of the mortar and howitzer, for it fired its projectiles in a high arc, which easily cleared the defences. Not only were stones or rocks fired, but also incendiary devices and rotting animal carcasses.

To batter through the wall, a catapult was used to hurl rocks at its surface. This engine, along with the ballista which fired large bolts or arrows, can be seen as the forerunner of the field gun, for it fired on a flat trajectory.

Another device often used was the battering ram. In its simplest form, this would be a tree trunk operated by a number of soldiers, who repeatedly dashed it against the surface of the wall. For the protection of the operators, battering rams were often wielded under the cover of a mobile canopy, called a 'sow' or a 'cat'. Sometimes the ram had an iron end attached, to enhance its effect against the wall.

Often, combinations of more than one device were used, such as a tower which incorporated a battering ram, and it should be borne in mind that quite often the defenders also had ballistas, catapults and mangonels at their disposal.

The only way under a wall was by mining, whereby the attacker sought to weaken the foundations of the defence work, either by making them collapse or blowing them up. The arrival of gun powder rendered the castle obsolete, for no defensive wall could withstand the impact of cannon balls for long.

Fortifications did not die out however and sieges continued. While the actual nature of the siege altered to match the changing defences, the general principles remained.

Other Methods of Siege Warfare

In spite of the somewhat complex defences and counter measures discussed above, starvation remained the principal siege weapon. Why risk your men in a costly assault, when all you have to do is to encircle the place and wait for the defenders to run out of supplies? There can be problems with this simplistic approach. To start with, the besiegers must have adequate supplies of food themselves in order to maintain the blockade. While initially they may be able to live off the surrounding countryside by foraging, it will not be too long before the forage parties have to roam further and further afield in search of supplies. Food convoys become a necessity and their safe conduct across what is probably unfriendly territory means involving a goodly number of troops. Guerilla attacks on convoys, on the siege lines themselves and the ever present possibility of a relieving army arriving on the scene all add to the problems of what is, at first glance, the 'easy' option.

Deception can also be used, and this follows two main themes. Someone inside the defences, either loyal to the attackers or who has been bribed, can work on the morale of the garrison. Also reports as to the state of supplies can be smuggled out, or further, the spy could perhaps arrange to have sentries over-powered at a set moment to assist the success of a surprise assault.

Trickery can also be wrought from without. One classic example is surely the famous Trojan horse. The Greek besiegers of Troy are reputed to have built a huge wooden horse which they then left outside the city gates one night. The defenders assumed that the horse formed some sort of appeasement and trundled the model into the city. Hidden inside the horse were Greek soldiers who crept out and opened the city gates to let in their waiting comrades outside. Granted, all this is partly legend, but before dismissing the idea out of hand, it is important to appreciate just how very much omens, portents and signs meant to ancient peoples. A battle would not take place if the soothsayers proclaimed that the gods were not in favour. This may all seem rather silly to us in the 20th century, but it was all very real to the ancient Greeks.

Other methods of subterfuge could also be employed. We have all surely read of the foreign legionnaires propping up their dead comrades at the ramparts of a desert fort in order to deceive the attacking Tuaregs into thinking that there were more men than was the case. In the American Civil War it was a common tactic to deploy tree trunks in besieging artillery positions. From a distance they looked just like siege guns and the hope was the defenders would surrender rather than face a heavy bombardment from all those guns.

Summary

The purpose of this section has been to underline both the suitability of sieges as solo wargames and the wide, sweeping variety which is available. There is no need to create a wargames army just to refight a siege. The chances are that there were several sieges in the period(s) that you already wargame, so the artillery which accompanies your army – whether it consists of catapults or field guns – can readily double as siege artillery. Granted, the object or recipient of the siege will need to be constructed, but this is fairly easy to achieve. Most wargamers can knock up some sort of effort to represent the required fortifications. Provided they are functional, that is all that really matters, but if the aesthetic appeal is important, then many suitable items are available commercially.

A Siege in More Detail

After looking at the general aspects of siege warfare and considering its undoubted wargames potential, it is now time to examine one particular siege in more detail. The period under consideration is the early 18th century, a period renowned for its sieges and a time when defensive works reached their peak of perfection. That the fortifications were so advanced was largely due to one Sebastien le Prestre de Vauban (1633–1707). Vauban's name is synonymous with the art of fortification and siege warfare. Based on geometric shapes designed to offer maximum defence and fields of fire to their defenders, Vauban's works grew increasingly complex in conception. Fittingly enough, Vauban was also a master of siegecraft and could apparently calculate to the day when the town or fortress which was under siege would fall.

The siege programme which follows is a typical example of an 18th century siege. It is somewhat irrelevant as to who is besieging whom, or for that matter the precise period. If the wargamer wishes to recreate a similar siege, fine. If not, then the general principles of what follows are applicable to virtually any period of warfare.

The siege has been described in chronological sequence, which has been itemised for easier reference.

STAGE 1 The first stage of a siege is that the fortress or town in question is totally encircled by its attackers. To achieve this, mounted patrols move on ahead of the main army and secure all

The author conducting a solo battle on his wargames table.

the roads in and out of the area. This prevents the defenders sallying out in attack and also prevents reinforcements arriving. This can prove to be an exciting part of the siege, with patrols of both sides coming into contact and brief skirmishes resulting.

STAGE 2 As a further defence against counter attacks from the garrison, a line of siege works is constructed, encircling the town or fortress. Usually these lines of contravellation consist of an earth wall with a ditch to its front. While these initial lines are being constructed – which can take a fair while, depending on the size of the place and the number of men available – the attackers are fairly vulnerable. Because these initial lines are constructed a fair way out, artillery fire and sorties by the defenders can cause casualties amongst those involved in the work.

STAGE 3 If the besieging commander feels that there is any possibility of a relieving army arriving on the scene to assist the defenders, then more siege lines are built, this time facing outwards. These lines of circumvallation as they are termed, are an optional extra and the wargamer can include or omit them as required.

The possibility of a relieving army does need to be considered. If the besiegers do not have the benefit of a covering field army, then the extra line of siege works is probably necessary. Should help arrive for the garrison, the besiegers may well find themselves trapped and assailed from two sides. Many major battles directly resulted from the attempts of commanders to raise a particular siege. Thus, in wargames terms, the potential presence of a relieving force does need careful thought.

STAGE 4 The besiegers then set up their main base of operations, either between the two sets of siege lines, or simply behind those of contravellation if that is all that has been constructed. Here are established artillery parks, ammunition dumps, food stocks and accommodation, usually under canvas, for the troops involved in the siege.

The quantities involved can provide the wargamer with plenty of logistical problems to solve. Really, a great deal depends on the amount of detail which the individual wishes to incorporate. A head count of the besieging forces and their daily consumption of say bread and meat can be calculated, as can the fodder for the horses. The amount of ammunition which is available for each type of cannon can also be stipulated, with, it should be stressed, reasonable figures being used. There is little point in allocating say a million cannon balls per gun. Not only is such a figure totally unrealistic, but it mars the whole concept of what we are attempting.

Similarly, the food and ammunition stocks held by the defenders can be monitored by the wargamer, who will thus have ample book-keeping to occupy his time.

STAGE 5 So, with a base firmly established, the attacker can set about selecting a likely looking site for his initial assault. This can be a projecting outwork, or bastion as they were called, or perhaps a smaller version of a bastion, termed a ravelin. It may be stating the obvious, but these outer defences have to be overcome before the central keep or citadel can be assaulted.

Figure 27

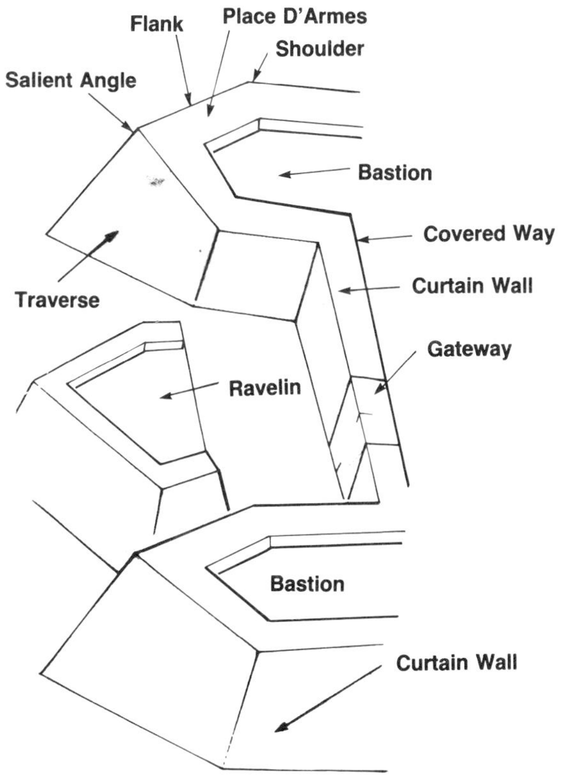

The relative positions of Bastions, Ravelins and other parts of a typical 18th century fortress.

STAGE 6 Once the site for the attack has been selected, stores are amassed near the area, in readiness, and batteries of siege guns are established in prepared positions. A trench is then dug to run parallel with the section of the defences to be attacked. To reach the appropriate site for this trench or parallel, as it was called, an approach trench has to be dug. Since it is constructed directly towards the enemy positions, this takes the form of a zig-zag, in order to prevent the defenders fire from sweeping down its length.

To minimise casualties as much as possible, the digging of such trenches was carried out under the cover of darkness, but such was the amount of work involved that trench construction could be a 24 hour a day task, so casualties amongst the working parties were inevitable.

This stage can also be quite lengthy and the wargamer may wish to calculate rates of progress. Much will depend on the nature of the ground, the attitude of those doing the digging and the liveliness of the defenders. The possibility of counter attacks by the garrison is ever present and they could perhaps be initiated by a random dice throw.

STAGE 7 Once the parallel trench has been dug, the pace of the siege hots up. Stores and men pour into the trench which acts as a forward base from which the besiegers press on with the assault. Artillery and mortar batteries are mounted and further zig-zag trenches are advanced towards the enemy as the process begins once more. The counter fire by the defenders will undoubtedly be heavy and the attackers will continue to lose men.

STAGE 8 Another trench is now constructed, nearer to the defences than the last, but again running parallel to them. Counter attacks by the defenders are extremely likely at this stage and some fierce mêlées can result.

For the third and last time, trenches are pushed out to the defences and yet another parallel is established. It is here that the as yet unused shorter ranged artillery will be sited to add their fire power to that of the heavier guns in an attempt to create a breach in the walls.

STAGE 9 It is now time to evict any of the defenders' troops who may be occupying the external, lower defences. This can be the section of the siege which causes the most casualties, but it is vital for the attackers to succeed. The situation also offers the

The residency at Lucknow, India, under attack during the Indian Mutiny of 1857. The building is scratch-built by Steve Woods, the 25mm figures are by Wargames foundry.

wargamer the rare opportunity to use grenadier figures for once. It is these men, who, supported by artillery fire until the last moment, are tasked with forcing the defenders from their positions.

Fierce indeed are the mêlées here and the usual morale rules are best waived in this situation, if the assault is to be in any way realistic. The first troops into the defences were often promoted on the spot, such was the grim nature of the combat.

STAGE 10 Once the external defences are seized, siege guns are then sited there. The effect of heavy shot at close range quickly finishes off weeks of work and a breach in the rampart wall soon appears.

STAGE 11 Once the wall is breached the final assault can take place. In front of the rampart wall however is usually a ditch, either dry or filled with water. A temporary bridging is achieved by the use of fascines – bundles of tree branches tied together, as one after the other is dropped into the ditch.

STAGE 12 When all is ready and the ditch is bridged, the grenadiers are once more sent in to storm the breach in the wall.

Here more fierce hand to hand fighting takes place as hopefully – but not necessarily – the attackers carry the day.

Final Points

The defenders may, at any point in the siege, surrender and should be afforded the honours of war – allowed to march out with flags flying and carrying their muskets. Should the defenders not surrender, then the consequences could be frightening when the attackers did finally overcome the defences.

Once the walls were breached it was not necessarily the end of things, for the citadel or keep had still to be taken. However, if the outer defences had gone, the citadel often surrendered. If they did not, short range fire from the heavy guns which the attackers could now freely deploy would soon weaken the walls. Another assault by the over-worked grenadiers might be needed before the citadel capitulated, but the final outcome was never really in question.

Summary

The siege wargame then, offers the solo player a feast of ideas and situations to explore. Indeed, if conducted on a 'real time' day to day basis, the siege can take on a life of its own, with the wargamer simply moving figures and book-keeping as required.

9 POSTAL WARGAMING

This chapter sets out a brief explanation of the possibilities and the mechanics of wargaming with opponents who may be hundreds of miles away. There are several methods of conducting wargames by post and these will be discussed later, but what they all have in common is to provide a regular contact between wargamers who are geographically remote and who would not otherwise be able to share their hobby with one another.

Postal wargaming lends itself to campaigning with strategical moves, orders, tactics, order of battle etc. all being communicated by post rather than directly across the wargames table.

So, having established that postal play is essentially not dissimilar to 'regular' wargaming, other than the distance between the participants, we can now examine the 'pros and cons' of this aspect of wargaming. On the plus side is the fact that campaigns and games can be conducted between players who could not otherwise play against one another. Regular contact is maintained and it should be borne in mind that while someone living in the UK can correspond quite happily with a person on the other side of the world, a wargamer does not have to be so far away before the Post Office provides the only regular contact.

Since inevitably some time elapses between moves, consideration can be given to both the strategical and tactical thoughts and theory behind a particular campaign or game. Indeed, the wargamer can indulge in the minutiae of war, details of military doctrines and theories, ordnance, commissariat etc. to an almost unrivalled degree.

There are possible disadvantages to postal play, just as there are to most things in life, but there is no face to face confrontation and the battles caused by the postal campaign can be successfully played out on one's own table, leaving the postal player still very much a 'one man band'. Part of a large multiplayer game perhaps, but still alone in the sense of discussing the game and the relative merits of a particular strategy.

There are also, as mentioned earlier, the inevitable gaps between moves – a minimum of a week for example, although this may be judged as being optimistic and a fortnight a more realistic time scale. The campaing can stagnate due to the time passing between letters and a great deal depends on the players' interest and involvement in order to maintain the momentum.

New postal wargames are usually announced in the play-by-mail type of magazine. The only publication of this type of any standing known to the author is *Lone Warrior*, the magazine of The Solo Wargamers Association which has a play-by mail section. The organiser, or 'gamemaster' as he is sometimes called, will advise the readers that he is organising a postal game and request interested parties to contact him at the supplied address. The initial mention usually only supplies the very basic information – 'J. Jones is organising a postal play game set in the late 16th century and requires six to eight players.'

Interested parties will then write to the organiser who will send out further details. Should the people wish to join in, then they usually have to pay an entrance fee for which they receive personality, command and strategical/tactical briefings. If the game is oversubscribed, then lesser commands and personalities can be allotted to accommodate more players. The organiser is the king-pin of such games, for it is he who designs and structures the game, decides who does what and generally controls the entire affair.

While the organiser or gamemaster can act as the umpire of the postal campaign the two jobs are not identicial. Not all postal games include an umpire – or a gamemaster for that matter – but in multi-player games he is a useful chap to have around. It is the umpire to whom moves in the postal game are usually sent and it is he who plots the results on a master map and records them in the campaign diary, so that one person at least has an overall appreciation of what is going on. By reference to his master map or the diary the umpire can establish what contacts have been made between the forces of the various players and advise the parties concerned. This may appear rather long-winded, but it does underline another element of war, the frustrating delay in order transmission and the way in which the situation changes before the participating players can react.

Multi-Player Games Whilst the gamemaster and even the umpire can be classed as luxuries in a game, the players are the essential component, for without them there is no game. Players in the larger games usually write directly to the gamemaster or the umpire with their moves and orders, but they may also need to write to one another direct. Depending on the style and period of the game in question, each player will have a personality to play and a command to look after, perhaps in a position subordinate to another player, or perhaps they will have a purely political role with no troops to worry about. If the gamemaster possesses a devious nature, the participants will have varying victory conditions set for them by him, usually unbeknown to the rest of the players. Postal multi-player games have a reputation for bringing out the very worst in the participants' character!

Two Player Games A two player game, lacking all the trimmings of the larger game, puts a lot more work onto the players themselves and often subsidiary rules have to be dispensed with. However, since there are just the two participants, the response time is reduced and the involvement is greatly increased, as is the sheer enjoyment. To a certain extent each player is his own gamemaster and umpire in that he sets his own aims and records both his own moves and those of the enemy on the map and in the campaign diary. When any decision has to be made the telephone is available if necessary, or the dice can be called into play. Battles as a result of the map contact can be set up on the wargames table in the usual way and played out as a straight solo wargame. Either both players play each game and take an average of the two results, or they take it in turns to fight the actions and inform the other player of the outcome. A degree of trust is obviously needed here, but it is a shallow minded soul who simply adjusts every table top outcome in his favour.

Solo Play An ideal situation for the soloist is the idea of solo play through the post. One wargamer may be conducting a solo campaign and as a result have a battle to fight through. In order not to affect his impartiality, all the relevant information can be sent to another solo player who then fights the battle and advises the 'campaigner' of the outcome. Many players enjoy playing solo set-piece wargames and to have them supplied through the post to play out and report on is a most useful stimulus.

Mechanics Having looked at the participants in a postal campaign, let us now see how the project can be organised. As with all things there are many methods, but what follows is a fairly representative selection.

The League Table This type of postal play offers another method of playing 'one off' battles rather than those created by a campaign. There are two variations on a theme here. Either the complete game is played through the post with each soloist submitting a move or sequence of moves as both players play out the game, or the scenario for the wargame can be created by one player for the other to play through. Two points are awarded for a win and one for a draw, and as a result in a group of postal solo players using this method a winner emerges. An umpire can be used and he will advise players as to their progress or even play out the entire game as a solo affair, using orders supplied by the two postal solo players.

The Campaign The campaign is probably the mainstay of postal wargaming. With any number of solo players taking part, such campaigns can, as we have seen in earlier chapters, embrace every facet of military action. In this type of game – and in the others for that matter – much depends on the dedication and reliability of the players. These are key factors in postal play, for if just one solo player lets the side down then the entire campaign is jeopardised. Campaigns can, and literally do, run until they are finished, with either the objectives of one army being achieved or maybe one side being so overwhelmed as to be forced to surrender.

The Mini Campaign The author has been taking part in a fairly long-running solo postal mini campaign with the noted wargamer Charles S. Grant. Set in the second half of the eighteenth century, it is a campaign of manoeuvre and position. While it is based on a fictional situation, we always try to make the campaign follow as closely as possible the methods of warfare prevalent in the period in question. Cities, towns and villages all have a points value for their possession so that as one army invades the territory of another, an indication of its success is given. Supplies are covered, as are troop drafts to replace casualties incurred by the various units involved. Each campaign day is divided into four moves and Charles and I take it in turns to send one another moves for our own forces on for example '*2nd quarter, 22nd July 1757*'. The moves are recorded in the campaign diary and the map squares which contain troops are also noted. The identity and strength of these troops is not disclosed unless a contact between opposing forces is established. We take it in turns to fight out any actions as solo battles on the wargamers table and inform the other as to the outcome, along with casualties sustained, colours lost etc.

Summary

An idea then of the potential of postal wargaming, what it involves and something of how it works. A short examination such as this can only serve to whet the appetite of the soloist and is probably more notable for what has been omitted rather than for what has been included. Nevertheless, it is hoped that this chapter has outlined the possibilities of postal play for the solo wargamer and how such a method can manage to achieve something of a paradox by involving more people and yet increasing the number of solo wargames available to the players.

10 THE SOLO WARGAMERS ASSOCIATION

No book on solo wargaming would be complete without a mention of the Solo Wargamers Association. The 'founding father' of the Association is John Bennett, a professional musician who from the very start of his wargaming interest in the early 1960s was intrigued by the methods used to design the wargame rules then in use.

It wasn't long before John was experimenting with his own rule mechanisms. The players who had previously been press-ganged into service for early 'conventional' games now became a distinct hindrance and were gently unloaded. Charts were used to simulate an invisible opponent's reactions and these were developed into rules that specifically required only one player.

John had no guidance for all this, as solo wargaming was badly neglected in the wargaming press of the day, but by 1970 or thereabouts a thought developed that there must be other wargamers with similar interests. The idea of forming some sort of solo wargamer's club was considered, but nothing came of it at this stage.

It was not until 1975 when a letter appeared in an issue of the now sadly defunct *Wargamers Newsletter*, seeking information on wargaming without an opponent, that John was finally spurred into action. The following month the same magazine published a letter from him in which he invited all wargamers interested in solo playing to contact him. The response was encouraging and clearly the first task was to publish some sort of newsletter, the title for which was easy to coin – *Lone Warrior*. The very first edition of this aptly titled publication came out in April 1976 and the first major step for solo wargaming had been taken.

At first it proved difficult to persuade people to contribute articles on their solo wargaming techniques and at one point John invented a surly character named 'Baxter P. Ferris' in order to stimulate controversy. Baxter had an outrageous habit of vehemently criticising everything John wrote (but never anything written by other correspondents!) Eventually Baxter's cover was 'blown' by an astute piece of detective work and he was allowed to retire gracefully.

Slowly the word spread and the Solo Wargamers Association, as it was now called, gathered in strength and interest. Many wargamers joined the ranks, showing that perhaps solo wargaming was beginning to emerge from its 'Dark Ages'.

Lone Warrior rapidly became a very readable and extremely stimulating exchange of ideas for solo wargaming methods, as members offered their own thoughts on varying aspects of solo play.

Currently the Association has a world wide membership, which is numbered in the upper hundreds and *Lone Warrior* has grown from eight pages to 40. From humble origins as the 'silent majority', the Association is firmly established as one of the most important organisations in the hobby today, thanks to both the initial and continuing efforts of John Bennett, its founder and editor of *Lone Warrior* for no less than 10 years.

At the time of writing, the current Secretary is Bill Farley and readers interested in joining the Solo Wargamers Association or seeking further information can write to him at 50 King Arthurs Road, Exeter, Devon, EX4 9BH but please remember to include a self-addressed envelope when doing so.

11 IN CLOSING

I hope this book has achieved its purpose in encouraging the reader to consider solo play as a very real wargaming option.

The permutations on the various suggested game mechanisms are virtually endless, a fact that ensures the solo player can surely never tire of the hobby.

The only limits are the individual's imagination and circumstances – campaigns are waiting to be fought, battles won and countries conquered – all power to your dice throws!

As far as the author is aware, there has only ever been one other book published specifically for soloists, *Solo Wargaming* by Donald Featherstone (Kaye & Ward 1973), now long out of print.

The details of other relevant books have been noted in the text as they have been mentioned, but the inclusion of the author's favourite wargame books may be useful to others for further reading.

Bath, T., *Setting up a Wargames Campaign* (Wargames Research Group 1973, 1987)

Featherstone, D.F., *Advanced War Games* (Stanley Paul, 1969)

" *War Game Campaigns* (Stanley Paul, 1970)

" *War Games* (Stanley Paul, 1962)

Grant, C., *The War Game* (A & A Black, 1971)

Grant, C.S., *Programmed Wargames Scenarios* (Wargames Research Group, 1983)

" *Scenarios for Wargames* (Wargames Research Group, 1981)

Wells, H.G., *Little Wars* (Arms and Armour Press, 1970, reprint)

Wesencraft, C., *Practical Wargaming* (The Elmfield Press, 1974)

Wise, T., *Introduction to Battle Gaming* (MAP, 1969)

Young, P. & Lawford, J., *Charge! or How to Play Wargames* (Morgan Grampian, 1967, Athena Books, 1986)

INDEX